Exmouth
Devon.
July 25th 1980.

Dear Miss Cooper,
Having read your letter in
the Daily mail about "mongrel dogs" I am
enclosing a photo of "Bella" now aged 11
years. We had her from a Mrs Rust
who looks after strays for the R.S.P.C.A.
We have always preferred to have a
mongrel, our last dog, and
we couldn't wish for a
take her place. She
dog, and we wouldn't
pedigree. Need I say
like to buy your
publiced

Yours
Rach

ARDMORE

...one and can turn his paw
to any task that comes to
hand. He is quiet, clean
and well mannered, highly
intelligent and loves to
please us. e.g. fetching
things, (practising the piano,
(we are music teachers!) etc.
Toby has mothered our black
Labrador bitch, Ram, since we
got her at 5 weeks old nine
years ago. He adores people
and children, in fact he
is a perfect gentleman.

We also have a yellow
Labrador, a retired guide
dog for the blind called
Bran. He is a big, ill-mannered,
beam. He is almost 14
Toby — Bran is almost 14
We've had him 5 years so
we put up with his loutishness
yes, you've weighed us up.
We are all dog lovers!!

A few years ago I
wrote a little book called
'Toby's Tale' for children it
is in manuscript, not good
enough for publication, but I
could let you have a copy
if you wish.
Toby must be 11 years

...obtain a homeless black
lab. They had none, but
there was Toby looking very
sad. He was very dirty and
covered in lice. However
we paid our 7/5- and took
Toby home, called in a vet
who supplied the delousing
soap & gave the necessary
jabs.

We have never regretted
our action. Toby is all
breeds of dogs rolled into
one

# Intelligent and Loyal

Jilly Cooper

Intelligent and Loyal

a celebration of the mongrel

with photographs by Graham Wood

Eyre Methuen

London

First published 1981
by Eyre Methuen Ltd
11 New Fetter Lane, London EC4P 4EE
Copyright © Jilly Cooper 1981
Photoset and printed in Great Britain by
Redwood Burn Limited
Trowbridge

To Maxine Green
with love

Contents

List of Illustrations

The dogs shown in the black and white photos
all of which were taken by Graham Wood
are as follows:

The sepia photographs are all captioned and are reproduced by courtesy of their owners, with the exception of the photographs on pages 186 and 188 which are reproduced by courtesy of the Imperial War Museum. The photograph on page 207 is of Barney Walton.

Acknowledgements

I am extremely grateful to the people who have helped me with this book. They include Major Eric Stones and Jack Winterflood B.E.M. of Battersea Dogs' Home, Clarissa Watson of the National Canine Defence League, David Taylor F.R.V.C.S. and Dr Christopher Dowling and Miss Angela Godwin of the Imperial War Museum. I should like to thank Beryl Hill for typing the manuscript and Amelia Sallitt for helping me wade through the mass of correspondence when it first came in.

I am also deeply grateful to all the owners who wrote to me so entertainingly about their mongrels. One of the saddest aspects of writing this book is that many owners have since sent me letters telling me their dog had died. If any owners did not alert me of their dog's death before the book went to press and their dog appears as being alive, I hope they will forgive me and accept my deepest sympathy.

The lion's share of my gratitude, however, must go to the following mongrels who made up the *dramatis canes* of the book. Some of them are merely listed below. Others also appear in the narrative either in the text or in photographs. But it is hearing about the exploits of all these dogs that has enabled me to draw what I hope is a comprehensive portrait of the mongrel. They include:

22 Sallies, 15 Patches, 15 Sams, 14 Sandies, 12 Judies, 12 Peters, 12 Tobies, 11 Bobbies, 11 Princes, 10 Susies, 9 Bens, 9 Kims, 8 Freds, 8 Lassies, 7 Blackies, 7 Bobs, 7 Brandies, 7 Scamps, 6 Candies, 6 Chums, 6 Dusties, 6 Rexes, 6 Trixies, 6 Whiskeys, 5 Barneys, 5 Flashes, 5 Ladies, 5 Mandies, 5 Simons, 5 Tims, 5 Tinas, 5 Trudies, 4 Bellas, 4 Bruces, 4 Glens, 4 Jacks, 4 Jets, 4 Laddies, 4 Laddys, 4 Majors, 4 Megs, 4 Paddies, 4 Pennies, 4 Pips, 4 Rips, 4 Skips, 4 Snappies, 4 Spots, 4 Suzies, 4 Teddies, 4 Tinies, 4 Trudies, 3 Andies, 3 Basils, 3 Besses, 3 Biggles, 3 Boris, 3 Bouncers, 3 Bullies, 3 Charlies, 3 Cindies, 3 Dans, 3 Emmas, 3 Gypsies, 3 Heidis, 3 Honeys, 3 Jaspers, 3 Jumbles, 3 Luckies, 3 Lucies, 3 Lulus, 3 Maggies, 3 Monties, 3 Panchos, 3 Rickies, 3 Rories, 3 Rusties, 3 Scatties, 3 Shandies, 3 Sherries, 3 Sidneys, 3 Simbas, 3 Stumpies, 3 Sues, 3 Tesses, 3 Tonies, 3 Tramps, 2 Benjies, 2 Bills, 2 Blues, 2 Bonkers, 2 Bosuns, 2 Boys, 2 Bretts, 2 Brunos, 2 Brutus, 2

Busters, 2 Buttons, 2 Chloes, 2 Chums, 2 Dingos, 2 Dougals, 2 Flosses, 2 Fredas, 2 Geordies, 2 Georges, 2 Jakes, 2 Janes, 2 Jens, 2 Jennies, 2 Jesters, 2 Joes, 2 Jumbles, 2 Katies, 2 Krugers, 2 Leos, 2 Maxes, 2 Midges, 2 Moxies, 2 Nickies, 2 Oonas, 2 Oswalds, 2 Pebbles, 2 Pippas, 2 Pixies, 2 Poppies, 2 Rags, 2 Rascals, 2 Rebels, 2 Rikkis, 2 Robbies, 2 Robertas, 2 Rosies, 2 Ruperts, 2 Samanthas, 2 Sapphos, 2 Shebas, 2 Smokies, 2 Sophies, 2 Spikes, 2 Tessies, 2 Topsies, 2 Toscas, 2 Twiggies; Ally, Araminta, Armstrong, Arthur, Atlas, Barbara, Barnaby, Basil Brush, Baxter, Be-Be, Beau, Bed and Breakfast, Benghazi Ben, Benny, Bernard, Bessie, Beth, Bilbo, Bimbo, Bitsey, Bonnie, Bonny, Boot, Bootsie, Boy Biddy, Bozo, Brackie, Brian, Brownie, Buddy, Butch Cassidy, Buzby, Caerphal, Caesar, Caezor, Camp, Capon, Cara, Cassie, Charlie-Girl, Charlotte, Chela, Chip, Chips, Chuffy, Chummy, Chummy Boy, Cindy Loo, Coffee, Coon, Craighsmuir, Cresswell, Crusoe, Cymri, Cyrano, Daisy, Daisy Bell, Dandy, Dansey, Del, Dick, Digby, Dilly, Dolores, Don, Don Juan, Doris, Drooby, Duffy, Dugie, Edwina, Effie, Errol, Erroll, Evans, Fan, Fancy, Fella, Fleck, Floppy, Flossie, Fly, Folly, Fortnum, Foxy, Friday, Frisky, Frumpy, Gamma, Gemma, Gretchen, Greyfriars' Bobby, Grundy, Gyp, Gype, Hamlet, Hanna, Hannah, Harriet, Hatter, Henry, Hetty, Honey Ball, Jack the Goat, Jacko, Jackie, Jan, Jass, Jason, Jayne, Jess, Jesse James, Jill, Jim, Jimmie, Jimmy, Jock, Joker, Josephine, Josh, Josie, Joss, Jubilee Jimmy, Julie, Juno, Kerry, Kimmy, Lass, Littlewood, Luke, Mabel, Mac, Many, Maria, Marion, Matey, Maybe, Micky, Mike, Miky, Miquette, Missy, Misty, Mitch, Mitzi, Mollie, Mopsey, Mubbs, Mutt, Nellie, Nero, Nigger, Nimbus, Nina, Nipper, Nobby, Nipon, Old Boy, Oophy, Ossie, Otis, Pal, Pandy, Pappy, Partly, Pat, Patrick, Peanuts, Pedro, Peggy, Penelope, Pettah, Pilgrim, Pinkie, Pongo, Poochy, Poodle, Potter, Price, Psyche, Python, Quarry, Queenie, Raffles, Raggy, Rajah, Rats, Rexie, Rickie, Rob, Rocky, Robyn, Roo, Roobarb, Rose, Rover, Ruffey, Rufus, Russ, Saba, Sacha, Sady, Samba, Sambo, Samdog, Sammy, Sara, Sarah, Scooby, Scruff, Scruffy, Seamus, Seeley, Shadow, Shamus, Shaun, Shelley, Sheila, Sian, Sid, Simon, Sinbad, Sintra, Skippy, Smokey, Smokeyjoe, Smudge, Snarler, Snoopy, Snowy, Soda, Sophy, Stacey, Stan, Suki, Sunny, Tahli, Tammy, Tanya, Tara, Teddy-girl, Tessa, Texas, The Major, The Motorway Dog, The Tyke, Tib, Tich, Tiffany, Tiger, Timmie, Timmy, Tiny II, Titty, Toby, Toby-Jug, Tocra, Tojo, Topsy, Topsey, Topsey of Testwood, Toto, Towser, Trigger, Trinder, Trix, Trubble, Trudy, Trudi, Tub, Tuffy, Tulip, Tully, Timmie, Tuppence, Twiggy, Twizzle, Vicky, Waggles, Waif, Watney, Weena, Whistle, Whiskers, Whisky, Whiski, William, Willie, Willy, Willoughby, Wimbledon, Yillah, Zade, Zam, Zip, Zoie.

I have tried to make the above list complete: I must apologise for any errors or omissions it contains and hope it may be possible to correct them in any future edition.

Intelligent and Loyal

The author and her mother with
some of their beloved mongrels.

Introduction

What is this life if full of curs, I have no time to stand and stare.

There were always dogs in our family. But the ones that stood out were two mongrels called Rags and Evans. Rags, a little russet-coloured rough-coated Terrier, belonged to my grandfather, who was a clergyman. As soon as the organ struck up the last hymn, Rags, who'd been waiting at the church door, would trot up the aisle to collect my grandfather and later stand proudly by his side as he talked to the departing congregation. Rags was, in fact, much better with the parishioners than my grandmother who preferred to read novels. On one occasion a local Lady Bountiful came to tea at the vicarage. Rags promptly made a bee-line for her, sitting at her feet, gazing beseechingly into her eyes, whimpering adoringly.

'I have a way with doggies,' she kept telling my grandmother smugly. 'They all dote on me.'

Alas, when she rose to leave it was discovered she had been sitting on a large bloody bone.

Another time my aunt surreptitiously added Rags's and the cat's names to the bottom of my grandmother's prayer list, so the entire Mother's Union was exhorted in a ringing voice to pray for Raggety Bones and Mewkins. In the photograph facing this page Rags can be seen lying on my mother's knee. She says he was not happy on this occasion. He smiled because he had good manners but, being a free-ranging spirit like most mongrels, he disliked being held down.

Evans, who belonged to my paternal grandfather, was extremely ugly. So ugly in fact that when, on the day he arrived, my grandmother proudly took him into the garden to be introduced to the gardener, the old man scratched his head and exclaimed, ''Eavens, Mum, 'Eavens! If that was my dog, Mum, I'd have named him after t' other place.'

1

Despite his hellish aspect, however, Evans had a lovely nature, and was so intelligent that he managed simultaneously to drink out of the lavatory and hold the door open with his tail so it wouldn't shut him in.

To my everlasting regret both Rags and Evans died before I was born, but such was the force of their personalities that I felt I knew them almost better than the succession of charming pedigree dogs who enhanced my childhood. When I married and we moved to Putney, and for the first time had a largish garden and lots of space, it seemed natural to get a dog. Just at that time, a reader of the *Sunday Times* wrote to me saying she bred English Setters, and asked if I would like a puppy. I accepted with alacrity, and so began one of the great doomed love affairs of the age. Maidstone, the Setter, and I adored one another almost to the disgraceful exclusion of everyone else in the world, but I couldn't control him and he created dangerous mayhem wherever he went. When he was six, we acquired a mongrel called Fortnum (of whom more later) misguidedly hoping that a companion might settle Maidstone down. In fact it pushed him completely over the top and he had to be destroyed a year later.

Perhaps subconsciously seeking to stop myself rushing out and buying another English Setter puppy, I acquired two more mongrels, Mabel and Barbara, in quick succession, and found myself the owner of a pack. Such was the power of their collective charms, that before I knew it I was a mongrel addict.

If you love something you want to learn more about it. When I had Maidstone, I bought countless books advising me (admittedly with little effect) how to rear, look after, train, breed and show an English Setter. Setters even had their own Year Book filled with self-congratulation and hilarious anecdotes.

I found, however, to my dismay when I went to the library, that hardly anything had been written about mongrels except for the odd work of fiction. No book was devoted to them exclusively, which seemed extraordinary when there are more than 150 million mongrels in the world. Most dog-guidance books either ignored them completely, or described them pejoratively as being ugly and unpredictable.

The Kennel Club bans mongrels and they are excluded from all major dog shows. They are also appallingly served by many of their owners. During 1980 Battersea Dogs' Home took in some 14,000 mongrels, most of them too ill on arrival to be saved, because no one had bothered to fork out a fiver to have them inoculated. In contrast with this vast number of mongrels, only about 4,000 pedigree dogs were taken in – and this ratio is ₒmore or less the same in dogs' homes throughout the country.

Poor mongrel! We live in an age which champions the under-dog. Over the last decade, we've had International Women's Year, the Year of the Child, the Year of the Disabled, Gay Lib, Black Power, Student Power and Flower Power – surely it's time for the Year of the Cur. Perhaps Nigel Dempster was striking a first blow in the campaign for Mongrels' Rights in a piece on 'In and Out' in the *Sunday Telegraph Magazine* in 1979, when he wrote that Battersea mongrels were 'In', and several very popular breeds of pedigree dogs were 'Out'. I decided to strike a second blow by writing this book in celebration of the mongrel, and calling it *Intelligent and Loyal*.

My main problem was how to research the subject when there was no available literature. I had talked my head off to most mongrel owners in Putney, but that wouldn't make a book. I needed world-wide information. My husband, not a great dog fan, heroically drafted this advertisement for *The Times* and the *Daily Telegraph*:

> 'Mongrels' Lib. Jilly Cooper is writing the definitive book on mon-grels. If you have one or know of one, information and photographs will be welcome. It is time mongrels got a fair deal.'

I had no great hopes of a response. My friend Tim Heald, while writing his excellent book *It's a Dog's Life*, had put a similar ad-vertisement in the papers, asking for good dog stories. He only received fourteen replies. I am afraid none of the stories were terribly good and several of the letters asked for money. But it seems that the emotive word 'mongrel' made all the difference and incredibly, within a few days, I was absolutely snowed under with material from mongrel owners all over the world, none of them asking for money. In addition, to my eternal grati-tude, the *Daily Mail* printed a similar message in letter form. The *Evening News* took up the story with a picture of my three dogs romping in the garden, and the letters started coming in by the sackful. They were funny, heartbreaking and touching at the same time. I have never enjoyed a correspondence more. There were letters from children telling me about their family pets: 'I'm writing to you about our mongrel Foxy who is an excellent guard dog, although fat because she's been spade.' There were letters written in spidery hand and covered in tear stains from old ladies writing about some little terrier mongrel who'd died before the war. The photographs they sent in were almost better than the letters. They showed faded sepia dogs lying in ham-mocks, or sitting at the wheels of ancient motor-cars, or wearing yachting caps, or just brandishing a wagging tail and behind as they disappeared out of the photograph.

Most owners seemed to resent bitterly the fact that other people, particularly the owners of pedigree dogs, looked down on their mongrels. They were convinced that mongrels were the best dogs, but repeatedly suppressed the depth of their affection and pride by making a joke of it.

'Missy is a small, mainly white, creature with black spots, and blodges of brown on her face,' wrote Richard Ingrams, the editor of *Private Eye*. 'She is fairly ugly, has sharp teeth, beady little eyes and a tendency to yap at the smallest provocation. She was meant to have a rough coat like both her parents, but as things turned out she is smooth. Despite these failings, everyone including me seems to be devoted to her.'

Looking at Missy bristling out of her photograph one can see exactly why.

Missy Ingrams

In similar vein was one of the first letters that came in written on blue card from a Mr and Mrs Roberts of Walthamstow describing their mongrel, Errol. Into the card they had slotted two photographs, 'One in colour, and one in black-and-white in order not to overglamorize Errol.' In fact, as we later found when we went to photograph Errol for the frontispiece, he was a dog whom it would have been difficult to overglamorize.

One of the joys of writing *Intelligent and Loyal* has been collaborating with Graham Wood, who took the photographs. We first met when he came to take my picture for the *Daily Mail*. We ended up next morning with frightful hangovers and a set of the best photographs of my mongrels that have ever been taken. It was only after we'd decided to do the book together that he let slip the information that he couldn't stand dogs, and was absolutely terrified of them. Like most great photographers, however, he was able to overcome his prejudice when necessary.

Throughout the book we have used his photographs extensively, but when I wanted to illustrate an anecdote about a dog that was dead or who lived abroad or too far away, or to include a mongrel snapshot that was so funny or splendid it could not be left out, we have used photographs sent in by the owners.

For me *Intelligent and Loyal* has been a labour not just of love but of adoration. I still like pedigree dogs, but, having discovered the charms of the mongrel late in life, I hope I will be forgiven for writing with all the obsessive fervour and bigotry of the newly converted. My only regret is that there was not room to use all the marvellous material sent in. I hope that Graham's

4

less rose-tinted approach will balance the book; that people will have as much fun reading it as we had putting it together; and that this book may help the mongrel to achieve some of the recognition for his special qualities that he deserves.

No one I know has summed up these qualities better than Hugh Walpole, whose mongrel Jacob was the model for Hamlet, in the *Jeremy and Hamlet* books.

'I have owned a great many dogs,' wrote Walpole, 'some of them very finely bred, very aristocratic, very intelligent, but none of them has ever approached Jacob for wisdom, conceit, self-reliance and true affection. He was a ghastly mongrel. I tremble to think of the many different breeds that have gone to his making, but he had Character, he had Heart, he had an unconquerable zest for life.'

1

Chapter 1

How to classify your mongrel

From earliest times the dog has been of service to man, guarding his cave, hunting with him for food, and giving him friendship. Gradually, to suit his own purpose, man started to breed specific types of dog to carry out particular tasks. He produced Mastiffs, for example, who were strong and brave enough to fight fiercely in battle. He bred a wolf-like sheepdog, the Alsatian, to frighten off any wolf that threatened the flock. As a double bluff, he even produced the Old English Sheepdog who looked like a sheep, so that when the wolf descended unsuspecting on the fold, he was routed by a great woolly monster. Man also needed fast dogs like the Greyhound and the Foxhound to hunt the rabbit and the fox, he needed Terriers to dig his prey out from their holes, and Spaniels to retrieve it from the undergrowth. As people had more leisure, Pekes, Pugs and other toy dogs were bred for decoration and companionship.

Because each of these breeds was needed for special duties, their value increased, and, as with all expensive things snobbery crept in. The breed dog became a status symbol, and greedy breeders with an eye to financial gain produced more and more breeds allegedly for different purposes. In fact they seem often to have been creating mere collectors' items. At the same time, a huge sub-culture of mongrels were still carrying on their doggy life unheeded, attaching themselves to various owners, or surviving by scavenging.

The word mongrel, which is pronounced with a flattened 'o' in the same way as *mon*key and fish*mon*ger, comes from the Middle English word *Meng* (to mix), and from the Old English word *Gemong* (a mingling). A mongrel is a dog of mixed blood, whose parents were not of the same breed, or of any breed at all. A breed dog, say an Afghan Hound, has parents, grandparents, great grandparents and great-greats going back for at least ten generations, who are all Afghans. The mongrel, on the other

1. The Vertical Shagpile: Profusely covered in long straight hair; eyes seldom visible; comes in all shapes and colours; very sanguine temperament.

hand, is usually the product of many generations of chance matings, and may have as many as sixty breeds in his make-up.

To complicate matters the term 'mongrel' not only applies to a dog whose parents are both mongrels, but also to a dog whose parents are both pure bred dogs, but of different breeds. Therefore if an Alsatian mates with an Afghan, the puppy can either be described as a 'crossbreed', or an 'Afghan/Alsatian cross', but is still a mongrel because it is not pure bred. Equally if a Greyhound mates with a mongrel bitch, its offspring can be described as 'Greyhound crosses', but are still mongrels.

Many people tend to label all mongrels euphemistically but inaccurately as 'crossbreeds'. 'Mutt', 'tyke', and 'cur' are other less flattering names, as is the French 'Bâtard'. Americans and English owners often refer to their dog as a 'Heinz', because of the original 57 varieties. The Australians with typical down-to-earth humour call them 'Bitsers', because they are usually made up of bits of this breed, and bits of that.

As a large part of this book consists of anecdotes about various mongrels of all shapes and sizes, I have tried in this chapter to categorize them into types to make them more readily identifiable, and to save laboriously describing each dog's appearance when I came to it. If I have identified anyone's mongrel wrongly, I apologize; it is often difficult to tell exactly what a dog looks like from a small photograph. If your mongrel doesn't fit into any of the categories, you should be delighted: you are the privileged owner of a unique dog.

2

3

2. The General Wolfehound: Gentle giant of noble but slightly tousled appearance; coat shaggy but not woolly; comes in all colours.

3. The Romney Marshall: Medium length astrakhan coat, thick heavily-feathered legs; particularly prevalent in Kent.

4

5

4. The Woolly Whitejaw: Wiry astrakhan coat, white moustache and beard, elegant Angela Rippon legs; Poodle ancestry.

5. The Michael Foot: Lustrous long-haired red and white coat, long hairy ears set low on either side of head; qualities of leadership.

9

6 7

8 9

6.   The Borderline Collie:
Envelope flap ears, silky
luxurious coat, usually black and
white; curly tail optional; herds
anything – people included;
highly intelligent and intuitive.

7.   The Family Circler: Soft
longish coat in all colours,
envelope flap ears; will round up
family on walks and before meals;
supremely intelligent and loyal.

8.   The Twentieth Century Fox
Dog: Pointed ears and nose, long
bushy red fur and luxuriant tail;
bays like a fox at night; smooth-
haired version comes in other
colours and has tail without
feathering.

9.   The Ear Commodore: Comes
in all shapes and sizes;
distinguishing characteristic: one
ear standing to attention, the
other at ease; fearless, merry
nature.

10.   The Hover Cur: Smooth
hair; all colours but pale blond
preferred; coiled tail when static;
intensely agile; long-haired
version known as *Cross Channel
Furry*.

10

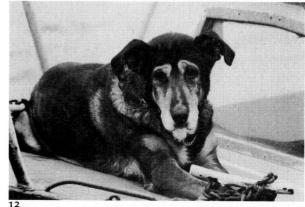

11 12

13 14

11.   The Spanish Policeman's
Hat Ear Dog: Distinguishing
characteristic: obtuse-angled ears
shaped like a Spanish policeman's hat; supremely loyal.

12.   The Old Sea Dog: Smooth
hair, usually black and tan, semi-
erect curling ears; distinguishing
characteristic: soulful black-
ringed eyes and square or
triangular widow's peak on
forehead; Alsatian ancestry.

13.   The Miniature Magpie:
Smooth close-cut white coat with
jet black patches; jaunty nature;
larger version known as *Standard
Magpie*.

14.   The Pied Wagtail: Slim
build; smooth, flecked black and
white coat; continuously wagging
tail.

15.   The Jack Russell: Believed
by many people to be a pedigree
dog but not recognized by the
Kennel Club because of the
number of variations in colour,
size and form. Small v-shaped
drooped ears, smooth but slightly
woolly coat; white with black or
tan markings; intensely
individual, sometimes
contentious; doughty hunters;
highly intelligent.

12

15

16

17

18

16. The Prop Forward: Smooth coat; solid compact body, barrel-chested and heavily muscled; boundless energy (particularly sexual); gladiator of the mongrel world. All colours.

17. The Black and Tan Tightskin: All shapes and sizes but coal black with rich red markings preferred; self-drying, sleek coat worn very tight; extremely friendly.

18. The Lancashire Hot Pet: Smooth coat; curled semi-erect ears which flatten close to the head like a seal's when returning from a night on the tiles; white shirt front; deceptively small, slender frame; intensely brave, fiery nature.

19. The Edith Sitwell: Smooth hair, curly tail; excellent sitter.

14

19

21

20

22

20. The Bertrand Russell:
Rough-coated, slightly shaggier
version of Jack Russell; comes in
all colours; merry nature; highly
intelligent; terrier ancestry.

21. The Rough Diamond:
Medium-sized, heavily-built,
compact body; copious rough,
shaggy coat; sometimes
distinguished by white diamond
on forehead; all colours,
effervescent nature.

22. The Rough-and-Reddish:
Rough red coat, slim build,
medium sized; gentle nature;
possible Red Setter/Irish Terrier
ancestry.

16

24

23

25

26

23.   The Fetcher: Medium length silky hair, plumed tail; most common colours: ebony, gold or red; loves to retrieve balls or sticks and carry newspapers or shoes; charming manners; excellent with children.

24.   The Satin Crammer: Broad-chested; highly-polished short-cropped coat, free from all feathering; very powerful tail; most common colours: black, yellow or red; intensely amiable, incurably greedy; tendency to go grey around the muzzle early in life, worrying where next meal is coming from; Labrador ancestry.

25.   The Half Cocker: Solid compact body, flat silky coat, long terry towelling ears; long tail preferred; comes in all colours; often identified by white blaze on forehead, widening over the muzzle; fifty per cent Spaniel parentage; jolly nature (but mind of own).

26.   The Headless Hound: Very economical to feed.

17

Chapter 2

The rescued mongrel

Oh rest ye, brother mongrels, we will not wander more.

'Lucy Nicholas joined our family in 1964,' wrote a friend when she learnt I was gathering material for a book on mongrels. 'My mother bought her out of sheer embarrassment when she came up for auction at a local Conservative party sale. As the auctioneer pointed her out as lot four, a piglet-like creature in an old cardboard box with a head too big for her body, the room fell silent. As the silence continued, my mother felt herself blushing at the humiliation the small creature must be feeling. When finally the auctioneer failed to raise a single bid, she gallantly offered £2 10s. and found herself the owner of the obvious runt of the litter.'

Lucy's new owner displayed that quixotic streak of compassion which I am proud to think of as peculiarly English. It is that same streak which sends thousands and thousands of people off to dogs' homes every year to rescue mongrels that are about to be put down. It is also that streak of compassion for the underdog among underdogs that often makes them, on reaching the dogs' home, choose the ugliest, most pathetic dog they can find.

Brutus Collis, a black-and-white Shagpile from Dorking was rescued from the local RSPCA home. According to his master, 'It was love at first sight. I saw Brutus trying not to look too eager to be picked out.'

'Simon's body was a bundle of bones and scabs,' wrote another owner. 'He gazed at us from a pile of straw, and when we didn't take him, he slunk back into the corner dejectedly so we changed our minds.'

'The dogs were all barking and throwing themselves against the bars,' said Mrs Chatwin of Orpington, 'except one misshapen black and tan bitch who was just sitting staring into

Lucy Nicholas

19

space with a hopeless, despondent look in her eyes. I knew instinctively this was the dog for us. She'd been thrown from a car and didn't trust anyone. However, she immediately jumped into our car as though she'd been in it all her life.'

Sometimes a prospective owner needs just a flicker of recognition to take on a particular dog. 'The local RSPCA shelter was full of beautiful breed dogs,' wrote Miss Woodrow of Gwent, 'but in one corner cowered a sandy mongrel bitch who'd obviously been ill treated. She gave my hand a lick and that was it – she cost us ten shillings.'

Ricky Lynne

Mrs Lynne of Upminster, however, preferred the grand gesture. 'The dogs were penned in twos and threes when I arrived. They were being given their only meal of the day. Ricky left his food to come and talk to me, that was that. He has grown into the most beautiful dog, and is loving to the point of adoration.'

Shelley Barton, a handsome cross between a Boxer and a Great Dane, both highly sensitive breeds which need a huge amount of affection, was obviously miserably displaced in the dogs' home, and on seeing her future mistress for the first time hurled her not inconsiderable weight into her arms, as if to say, 'I belong to you, please take me away from this terrible place.'

Certainly visiting a dogs' home is a gruelling experience – all those desperate creatures clamouring for attention. For the tender-hearted it is hard not to come away with a whole pack. Charles Dickens, for example, was upset by a trip to Battersea in 1862:

> As you come within sight of the cage, twenty or thirty dogs of every conceivable and inconceivable breed rush towards the bars, flattening their poor snouts against the wires, and ask in their own peculiar and most forcible language if you are their master or no.

A German, Dr Carl Schneider, visiting the home at the turn of the century, was even more upset, and was haunted for years by the vision of one particular stray:

> He looked at me with human eyes, whimpering and whining and unfolding his trouble to me in exquisite dog language, moving his body and tail in every conceivable posture of entreaty and abject submission, and when I moved away he pressed his nose and paws against the railing and emitted a cry such as might burst from the shipwrecked on a barren island, who sees the sail, on which he built his hopes of deliverance, disappear on the horizon.

20

It is the same today. There are few more heartrending sights than a van full of terrified strays arriving at the dogs' home. Once they are unloaded, their collars – the last vestige of their individuality – are removed and replaced by a Battersea collar with a number: regulation prison uniform, for prisoners who have not committed any crime.

But all dogs who enter here need not abandon hope. Of the 14,151 mongrels taken in by Battersea in 1980, 1,665 were reclaimed and a huge total of 6,451 dogs found homes. This admittedly means that around 6,000 mongrels were put down, but the majority of these were severely ill on arrival, either very badly injured in road accidents, or so diseased that they would have risked infecting the other dogs.

Battersea is only one of thousands of dogs' homes all over the country which are constantly placing dogs with new owners. The Canine Defence League, for example, takes in between 3,000 and 4,000 dogs a year and manages to rehouse 90 per cent of them. Another cheering aspect of dogs' homes is the dedication with which the kennel staff look after their charges, and the real satisfaction they find in returning a lost dog to its owner, or in placing a stray in a new home. As a rule, after a mongrel has been a certain time at Battersea, and the kennels are becoming overcrowded, he has to be put down to make way for other dogs only just come in. Fortunately the kennel maids get very attached to some of the less outwardly attractive dogs and keep moving them to the back of the queue. A dog called Old Boy, for example, stayed at the home for eleven months. He was an old mongrel nobody wanted: good-tempered, healthy, loved by the staff, but one who didn't, because no visitor showed any interest in him, go out of his way to sell himself any more. Everyone seemed to want a young dog, or a dog with a sad, appealing face. Happily the press got to hear of Old Boy's plight and published his picture with a story in the paper. Battersea was inundated with requests to adopt him: the quixotic streak of the English was at work again and he found a marvellous home.

Other mongrels are not so lucky as Old Boy. Miss Tanya Leonard, who works in a dogs' home near Newport Pagnell, cannot help getting attached to the strays she looks after.

'There was a little black mongrel we called the Motorway Dog, because he was picked up on the M1, obviously dumped. He had bleeding feet, a burn on his nose, and scars and scabs all over him. Some of the scars indicated that he'd been thrashed with a thin stick. It was really satisfying seeing him gain confidence and fill out. Four weeks after he arrived another dog

21

whom we called Basil, came into the kennels. We don't name all the dogs, only the ones for which we feel a special affection. Basil was terribly thin (I only once saw a dog so skinny, and that died) and surprisingly at first he refused food, but I took him out with me at lunchtime and gave him bits of my sandwiches. He enjoyed this extra attention, and gradually gained weight. He was such a happy dog, who wagged his tail for even the smallest thing.

'Both the Motorway Dog and Basil are fine examples of dogs who, if given the chance, will do anything to please, and despite an unhappy cruel past develop a beautiful individual character. But thanks to selfish people who are unprepared to look beyond the outside skin of a dog, and not at its personality, these dogs were put down last week. Both were well on the way to recovery, and looked forward to leading healthy, happy lives. I have put a brave face on it at work, but no one can tell me mongrels are not as good as pedigree any day.'

Sally Hart

It must be heartbreaking for the kennel staff to nurse a dog back to health, and then have to destroy him because he does not appeal to any prospective owner. Mrs Hart of Taunton, on the other hand, is just the sort of saviour the dogs' homes are looking for. She went to Somerset RSPCA and specifically demanded a dog no one else wanted. She was immediately given Sally, a four-year-old Rough-and-Reddish, whom everyone had passed over, despite 'eyes like clear brown trout pools', because she looked so commonplace. She had already been chucked out of two families, the first because the wife couldn't stand dog hairs, the second because she fought with the resident Cairn.

Not all strays come from dogs' homes, of course. Lucky Draper, a red Tightskin was found in a field in Northamptonshire.

'My grandfather,' wrote Lucky's mistress, Rebecca, 'was feeding the cows when he saw a car stop, and a man throw some rubbish over the hedge, and then drive off. Feeling furious, my grandfather drove his tractor over to pick up the mess, and found a puppy, very small and weak, all tangled up in her collar and lead, and almost dead with cold because it was snowing. Pop took her home, gave her some warm milk, wrapped her in a blanket and sent for Dad and me. Mum didn't have any say in the matter. She didn't want another dog, but she loves Lucky now (sometimes).'

Lucky Draper

Another little mongrel, called Matey Webb, was also found in the snow, tied shivering to a gate by a bit of string. 'We knew he wanted to live with us, when he didn't wee in the car going home. We washed him in the sink with Fairy liquid and wrapped him in an old blanket.'

Sometimes a rescued dog can cause dissension in a family. Mr Baines wanted a Great Dane, his wife wanted a Dachshund. Instead she found Sam, a tan and white Prop Forward, careering, obviously lost, through Bromsgrove, and brought him home. Mr Baines was incensed when he saw Sam *in situ*, saying he hated cringing dogs, and Sam must go at once. For the next week, Sam was secreted in an old cowshed like some prisoner on the run, but fortunately won his spurs the following week, when some neighbouring cows strayed onto Mr Baines's land. Sam promptly rushed out, rounded them up and drove them back. He returned to the house in triumph with a beaming master at his side.

'This is a simply marvellous dog, not like that other one,' said Mr Baines. 'Where on earth did you find him?'

Success with one stray tends to make owners take on another. Mr Byatt already had a beautiful Satin Crammer, another Sam, whom he'd bought for £5. Shortly afterwards he discovered a brindle Twentieth-Century Fox Dog in his garden who was limping badly and eating chip paper, because she was so desperately hungry. It took an hour of coaxing and throwing titbits to get her to lick Mr Byatt's hand and snuggle up in his arms. When he finally got her into the house, she slept for forty-eight hours.

In a nation of supposed animal lovers, it is utterly horrific to find that people can be so desperately cruel to dogs, dumping them in icy fields, or chucking them out when they go on holiday. The ultimate in heartless brutality, however, must be buying a dog for a child as a Christmas present and, when the child gets bored with it, dumping it on the motorway. One can imagine the panic-stricken terror of the wretched animal as it weaves desperately in and out of the oncoming traffic, seeing all it knows and loves fading as the number plate disappears out of sight. One's heart bleeds for Kim Crook III, a Jack Russell, who was discovered on the edge of a main road, creeping pathetically out of the verge to look hopefully at every passing car, then darting back again. Poppy Smerdon, a glorious Satin Crammer, was dumped by some gipsies on the A40 and taken to the nearest dogs' home.

'She clearly found us appealing when we saw her at the home,' writes her present master, 'and was determined we should be her new owners. My wife and I had been invited to a lunch party, and we took Poppy away but left her in the car. Obviously she felt left out, because she pushed down the window, and joined the pack of Labradors on the lawn. Since then we have not been parted from her. She is quite simply the best dog we have ever known. My wife and I and our two children, the cat and the tortoise are simply devoted to her.'

At other times the bond between mongrel and new owner is forged more slowly. Mrs Saunders of Liss, Hampshire, used to walk her Alsatian bitch in the woods every day, and was often trailed by a brindle Prop Forward, who was obviously a stray, whom she called Buster. Very nervous at first, he gradually over a year allowed her to talk to and then to stroke him. After that he followed her home, and for two days stayed in the garden.

Buster Saunders

'I fed Buster, but wouldn't let him in. He slept on the back doorstep, and cried to come in. Finally I weakened. No one seemed to have lost a dog, so he stayed. I think he'd been dumped by someone who had driven off. Whenever I started the car in the early days, he would rush and hide. He is rather noisy at times, but very loyal and affectionate.'

Some dogs – the quixotic streak at work yet again – are lucky enough to be rescued from cruel owners. Poor Patch Mellor, a Standard Magpie, was tied to a tiny box in a field for more than two years. Mrs Mellor used to take her own dogs for walks past him, and throw him pellets of bread and meat which often, alas, landed too far away for him to reach.

'He was a bag of bones, his white fur was yellow as though it had been singed (which the vet said was lack of nourishment). We finally approached the owner, who said in amazement, "Dost want him?" We took him straight away. He is about nine or ten now but plays like a puppy.'

Another philobrutist, Miss Jane Howell of Charlbury, was working in a café for pocket money when she discovered a little dog tied to a chair in the back room, who used to be pelted with bits of gristle and sausage meat at mealtimes.

'He was called Whiskey. I loved him at once with an enormous sense of outrage. The owners wanted an Alsatian, so poor Whiskey was for the chop. I bought him from them on the never-never, paying with my wages each week, and took him home on a length of washing line. I stopped on the way to let him loose in a meadow full of wild flowers. He'd never seen grass or sky, never been off a chain since he'd left his mother, and he went berserk. His back legs were weak through insufficient food, his back dipped through months of cowering, but he just ran and ran, leaping back through the buttercups to check I was still there, then barking and chasing, rolling and

24

snuffling. I re-named him Jesse James. He was an inspiration to everyone who met him.'

In the same way, little Twiggy Kirby, the original Edith Sitwell dog, belonged to an old lady who never took her out and made her sit behind a chair all day. When her new mistress took her to the vet when she was eight months old, he said her paws were like a new puppy's and her hind quarters were quite bare where she'd sat on them all the time.

'I don't think she'd ever seen a bird before,' writes Miss Kirby. 'She is spellbound by them, and tries to climb trees to get a better view. We've now had Twiggy over a year, and we feel she is having her youth now.'

Almost worse than dumping a dog on the motorway is turfing out a bitch when she's heavily in pup. Cara Bagnall, an exquisite black and tan Spanish Policeman's Hat Ear Dog came from Harrow Rescue Centre. A week after she arrived at 5 a.m. on New Year's Eve she had twelve puppies. Ten lived, but as Mrs Bagnall had had only a week to build Cara up, she was like a skeleton.

For the next six weeks, the Bagnall family dropped everything, turning the study into a nursery, and taking it in turns to bottle-feed the puppies. As it took nearly two hours to feed them all, as soon as one person finished, someone else had to start. The Animal Rescue League helped Mrs Bagnall find homes for nine of the puppies, but she kept the tenth and called him Boy: 'Both dogs have completely settled in and we love them dearly.'

It is in fact this nursing back to health and confidence that forges the cast-iron link of devotion between the rescued dog and his owner. Bully Latchford came from Battersea in the 1920s and had a close-cropped white coat, black ears, baleful eyes, and a docked tail so his whole rear end wagged. 'He had been terribly maltreated,' writes Mr Latchford. 'Weals across his back, and a raw mark on his neck from a too-tight chain. Every bone in his body stuck out. My mother was the one who nursed him back to health, I've never seen an animal show so much gratitude or intelligence.'

Some dogs are so badly treated that even with kind owners they never fully recover their confidence. Judy Manser, a black and tan Terrier Cross from the RSPCA, was still a mass of sores when she came to her new home. As her previous owners used to stub their cigarettes out on her, she still jumps a yard if people approach her suddenly.

My own Fortnum, our senior dog, was also the victim of ap-

Battersea dogs arriving

palling sadism. As a tiny puppy he was found hanging by wire from a branch – a gang of louts were staging an execution. The social worker had rescued him in the nick of time, and later handed him to a woman who believed her children ought to be brought up with animals, without liking them very much herself. While she was out at work, he was left in the house, and used to howl and annoy the neighbours. I met him on the way to the dogs' home. He was a slim brindle Prop Forward with anxious black-ringed Alsatian eyes who jumped up and licked my face when I admired him. I rushed home and rang my husband to ask if we could have him, and received an extremely irate lecture. Why the hell did I want to add to my problems, he demanded, when I already had five cats, a depressed goldfish, and one Setter whom I couldn't control. Then with one of those staggering *volte-faces*, which make him so endearing, he suddenly said, 'I shall be extremely annoyed if that dog isn't waiting

26

for me at home when I get back this evening. He will be called Fortnum.'

So Fortnum arrived, plus a basket, an orange and blue knitted blanket, and two rag dolls.

'He'll whine for hours when I go,' said his mistress. In fact he whined for ten seconds, then settled in at once, rampaging up and down the stairs with Maidstone, our Setter, and endearing himself to everyone, including my husband, with his charm and merriment. It was only after a few months, as we shall see in a later chapter, that his deep insecurity manifested itself.

Most mongrels that have spent some time in a dogs' home need a refresher course in house training. If you take on an adult, warn the dog books, be prepared for a strenuous month of rehabilitation. As with fostering or adopting disturbed teenage children, you will need endless patience, love and perseverance, but if the rewards are slow in coming, they are even more satisfying in the end. For once again (just as mopping up puddles and coping with the devastation caused by a young puppy cements your love for the little creature) it is the work involved in restoring an adult dog's confidence and gradually winning his love that binds the rescued mongrel and his owner so completely to one another.

Mrs Salvin of Minehead wrote that she had taken on three mongrel strays in her time, and found them all difficult at first. Buddy, left behind by an American soldier after the war, moped terribly, and wouldn't respond to any kindness for a long time. Peggy, a Rough and Reddish just saved from the gas chamber and brought home on a piece of string, was desperately uneasy and impossible to house train at first, but lived for seventeen years and in the end turned out wonderfully devoted.

Topsy, her third dog, a blond Romney Marshall, was turfed out on the street for having a litter in a coal hole (her owner hadn't even realized she was a bitch) and ended up at the RSPCA. She was so depressed she didn't bark for two months, but has now grown into an enchanting little dog, and shadows Mrs Salvin everywhere.

It took Mrs Webb of Hereford a year to rehabilitate Sally, her black, tan and white Tightskin: 'She was cowed, starved, and her coat was filthy and harsh to the touch like a moth-eaten scrubbing brush. She had fleas, mange, lice and was terrified from previous beatings, but she put a trusting and appealing head in my hand and with a quailing heart I took her home to see what I could do.

'Although obviously starving, she refused to eat or drink. I tried everything, but there was no response except an ominously curling lip. Eventually, in despair, I threw her my breakfast bacon rind, which she caught and ate. I realized she'd never been offered food in a bowl before. From then on I started to win. Although there were many days of frustration when the idea of returning her to the RSPCA seemed very attractive, I'm so glad I battled on. As you can see now, she's a sleek contented dog.'

Mrs Hart likewise needed great patience before she could win over Sally, the mongrel with eyes like trout pools, whom no one else wanted. Sally barked all the way home in the car, and on her first walk ran away, and stayed out all one wild and stormy night lying outside her old home.

'Gradually,' writes Mrs Hart, 'she came to accept us, until one never-to-be-forgotten-day she actually pulled back when a friend was taking her from me. The only sign she gave of remembering her original owners (who had a young baby) was hopefully peering into any pram that she passed, but she never ran away from home again and died at seventeen completely one of the family.'

One of the constant fears of the owner of a rescued stray is that the dog may suddenly find his former owner, and be reclaimed or at least long to go back. Pebbles Hudson, a little Black and Tan Tightskin rose from rags to riches when she left Battersea Dogs' Home and went to live in a mews house with the retired general manager of Shell. Pebbles now drives around in a Rolls-Royce, and has the distinction of being the first dog ever to be bought a first class inter-city ticket to Bristol, riding there in splendour on her own seat. Although she obviously adores her new master, it twists his heart that after a year she will still follow anyone who passes in the street, hoping perhaps that it might be her lost master.

Other dogs, in contrast, seem totally unaffected by their dreadful past. Biggles Kelly was adopted from the Sale RSPCA in 1979.

'We were taking a risk,' writes Mrs Kelly, 'as he had a frightful skin disease and had obviously been ill-treated, as he had rope burns round his neck and three broken ribs. Over the next three months, he healed up and became a beautiful dog, with a very even temperament. He has never tried to bite anyone.'

Another ugly dogling who grew up to become one of the most beautiful mongrels we photographed was Bob Gray, the original General Wolfehound. Bob was rescued by the local vet. Apparently his fiendish previous owners had moved away and

28

Pebbles Hudson

left him locked in their flat. It was three weeks before he was found, with no food, and just water from the lavatory to drink.

'When I saw this poor skinny thing,' said Mrs Gray, 'with bald patches, a big bandage on his tail, and frightened of everyone except the vet's assistant, my heart went out to him. After all, I'm hardly likely to win Miss World, so why should I expect my dog to look like a Cruft's champion?

'We had a few problems to start with. He wasn't house-trained, didn't understand any commands, and was so excitable he nearly wrecked the house and car in his efforts to protect them from burglars. He broke the window of the porch when someone called, and, when the road sweeper went by with his broom, knocked the rear window straight out of the back of the car. Fortunately this was all a big bluff. He has in fact a very gentle nature, and has grown into a most handsome, healthy and loving companion.'

One of the arguments breeders and dog books put forward against taking on a young mongrel (parents unseen) is that you never know how large or unprepossessing an adult the dog will turn out to be. They underestimate the strength of feeling most mongrel owners have towards their dogs, which is based on something much deeper than looks, so that even the drabbest dog, once acquired, will seem lovely. As La Bruyère wrote: 'If a plain woman succeeds in being loved, she will be loved passionately, for charms less obvious but far stronger than those of beauty.' It is the same with dogs.

29

Mrs Fasler of Birchington, Kent, seems to epitomize this love. 'I always get the dogs other people don't want. I told my husband this new one was the ugliest dog I'd ever seen. I had to take her because I'd raised her hopes, but I was going to call her Ugly. After a week I didn't think she was ugly at all, so I re-named her Rosie after certain chocolates that grow on you. She has turned out to be the most lovable mongrel one could find.'

The rescued mongrel has no birthday. Most owners give him an official one like the Queen. He has no parents, so speculation about his forebears is endless and fascinating, but quite un-profitable. Although his owners probably admit secretly that he is not the most classically beautiful dog in the world, they are fiercely protective, and long for other people to admire him. Over the past six years I have hoarded the few compliments Fortnum has received like a miser. They include:
'Intelligent and loyal.'
'Nice broad 'ead.'
'Looks a strong dog.'
'Oo could 'urt 'im, when they're all so lovely, in't they?'
'All muscle, isn't he?'
'Nice teef' (really scraping the barrel).
'Nice silky ears' (ditto).
'Look at his little frown.'
'Nice size.'
'Nice dog.'
'You can't miss 'im.'
'What breed is he?'

Just as owners of pedigree dogs often keep in touch with the breeder, telling her how her former charges are getting on, owners of strays often forge a link with the past by writing to the dogs' home from which they've acquired their dog, giving a report of its progress. Battersea has some marvellous letters from satisfied customers, usually signed with a muddy print.

'Dear Sirs,' wrote Emma. 'Three years ago, my grandmother, my mother and I came to Battersea Dogs' Home, and came away with Jason a lovely mongerell. He is in cracking form, and as fit as a hunter. He is also the best companion I have ever had. I often see him guarding my seven-week-old sister's pram, and sometimes he knocks my two-year-old sister over, but she doesn't like it much. His hairs are gharstly because he is molting now. Still I am very thankful we came that day.
P.S. Jason sends a great slobery kiss.'

Bonkers O'Shea

Since Mrs O'Shea acquired Bonkers, a golden Fetcher, from Battersea, she's never had a dull moment either.

'I had put an old burnt-out kettle in the hall,' she writes, 'and forgot about it. In the middle of the night I was woken by a terrible rattle – it was Bonkers flying from room to room, banging against everything in his path. He now has two kettles he bangs and takes to bed with him. He likes to leap into cars and kiss men drivers, and pinches those yellow plastic cones they put along the road, and also cardboard boxes, and brings them home. I sometimes wake up at four o'clock in the morning to find him stretched across me, legs in the air, nose in my ear, bedclothes all over the floor.'

Chapter 3

Intelligence

Nine out of ten dog guidance books will assure you there is absolutely no evidence that mongrels are more intelligent than breed dogs. Why, they demand scornfully, are there no mongrels in the army, or the police force, or taking part in sheep dog trials? They then attack the mongrel supporter for always drawing his conclusions by comparing an unusually bright mongrel with an exceptionally stupid breed dog. One must concede that there are some brilliant breed dogs, and equally thick mongrels. But there has also been pitifully little research into mongrel intelligence or even mongrels at all, compared with the vast literature devoted to breed dogs.

In championing the mongrel, I can only stress that out of approximately 1,500 letters sent to me, the huge majority of writers emphasized their dog's intelligence, giving endless examples of which only a tiny handful can be illustrated in this chapter. In numerous letters, too, owners spoke of the revelation of keeping a mongrel for the first time, after previously owning only breed dogs, and how much the mongrel exceeded them both in brains and empathy. Others noticed that when a mongrel moved into a house already inhabited by breed dogs, it would be ruling the roost in next to no time.

I suspect the bias against mongrels stems not only from insufficient research, but also because most dog guidance books are written by three kinds of people: first, the breeders who have a vested interest in playing down mongrel intelligence; second, the vets, who are irritated because mongrels have that inbred aid to health known to scientists as 'hybrid vigour' and are therefore unremunerative patients; and third, the dog trainers who find mongrels difficult to teach because they have minds of their own and refuse to follow instructions slavishly. When parted from his owner and left with a trainer, the mongrel tends to pine and be unresponsive. On the other hand he learns quickly from his owner, because he's so anxious to please.

33

Sam Williams

One reason there are no mongrels in the police or the army is because they don't instantly symbolize authority. If you are about to start a riot or bash up an old lady, you're more likely to think again if an Alsatian or a Rotweiller comes pounding round the corner, rather than a lovable mongrel, however intelligent.

One senior policeman attached to the Hampshire force, however, did realize the full idiosyncratic potential of the mongrel, and decided to inject a note of comedy into the routine police dog displays. About six years ago he sent for PC Williams, one of his most experienced dog handlers, and told him to find a really scruffy but intelligent mongrel. Somewhat sceptically PC Williams set about this task and, having drawn a blank at all the local dog sanctuaries, took a train up to London to visit Battersea Dogs' Home.

'I sat down in this big compound,' said PC Williams, 'and lit my pipe, and had a good look at all the dogs that were milling around. Sam was the first one to come up and introduce himself. He was certainly one of the scruffiest, dirtiest animals I've ever seen, but he was also the most delightful, and although soon other dogs followed suit and came up and talked to me, I knew I couldn't go home without Sam.'

The only drawback was that once he got home, and was bathed and groomed at the police kennels, Sam turned into a very handsome dog, with merry amber eyes, a magnificent brown and white coat, and a plumed tail like an ostrich feather. Fortunately for his future he was as brainy as he was good-looking, and still retained his essential mongrel insouciance. He was also exceptionally quick to learn. He needed to be.

Less than seven weeks later, a large crowd including the Queen and the Duke of Edinburgh were gathered at Stratfield Saye, watching a group of police Alsatians giving an immaculate obedience display. Suddenly a disreputable-looking individual dressed in a dirty mac and a flat cap, with a jaunty brown and white mongrel on the end of a piece of string, dodged under the ropes, and had the impertinence to line up with the other dog handlers. A voice over the tannoy warned him to make himself scarce. Immediately an over-zealous security man in a 'hundred and fifty guinea check suit' charged up to the disreputable-looking individual and tried to frog-march him out of the ring.

'Beat it,' muttered PC Williams under his breath, 'Sam and I are part of the act.'

Next minute, to the ecstasy of the crowd, Sam was taking part in the display. Following PC Williams' orders, he did every-

34

thing the other police dogs did, making up in exuberance any-thing he may have lacked in precision. Her Majesty and her husband were seen to be much amused.

So began Sam's remarkable career. Working alongside the police dogs, he took part in displays all over Hampshire, and stole the show wherever he went. When he did what he was told the crowd adored it, and if he occasionally slipped up, they enjoyed it even more. Alas, he was only allowed to delight his public for a year, at the end of which time, owing to the shortage of manpower, all police dog demonstrations were reluctantly discontinued. Poor Sam was forcibly retired and a shadow hung over his future. Luckily he had so endeared himself to PC Williams and his family by then that they adopted him as a family pet, and he is still keeping them amused by his antics.

Sam must have had more than a dash of sheepdog blood, which tends to make dogs both biddable and very easy to train. Before the Second World War, however, and for some time after, the most popular breed in this country was the Terrier. As there were more Terriers about then, the majority of mongrels seemed to have Terrier blood and, as a result, to be alert, argu-mentative, intensely individual, and absolutely bursting with character. Today when Labradors, Old English Sheepdogs, Yorkshire Terriers, Spaniels and Alsatians share the honours for the most popular breed dog, you will find most mongrels have more than a touch of one of these breeds in their make-up.

A typical example of the pre-war Terrier mongrel was Jacky Bowyer-Kairns, an adorable, mournful-eyed, brown and white Hover Cur found wandering through Bradford without a collar. Once shown a trick, Jacky knew how to do it. When told to shut the door, he immediately stood on his hind legs and banged it shut with his front paws. He would always bring the post up-stairs when it arrived, and rush off down-stairs to fetch the dustpan and brush if anything needed sweeping up.

'His praying was wonderful too,' writes Mrs Bowyer-Kairns. 'A sweet was placed on a stool, and Jacky would kneel well down on his front paws, one eye closed, the other open. Then you said, "Please make Jacky a good boy, let him go to heaven with his friends when he dies", and so on as long as you wanted until, at the magic word Amen, he would gobble up the sweet.'

Drooby Macdonald of Bromsgrove, on the other hand, a grey Vertical Shagpile with possibly a touch of Chow and Old English Sheepdog blood, is a fine example of a mongrel of the eighties. Drooby has a huge repertoire of tricks, and when asked can 'sit, smile, show his tongue, shake his head, bring his

Jacky Bowyer-Kairns

35

tail, lie down, roll over, kiss, whine "yes" when asked if he would like a biscuit or his dinner, give one paw then the other, do bottoms up, bare his teeth, sing and speak (bark). He can also fetch his ball, an old shoe, pussy (an old wig), knowing them all by name. If his mistress tells him she's going to the shops, he goes and lies down until she gets home.'

Suzy Evans of Clwyd, another modern mongrel – a Satin Crammer of obvious Labrador extraction – is very bright but in true mongrel fashion acts stupid when it suits her. According to her mistress, 'she knows what sit, stay, come home, go away, fetch, ball, squeaky bone, ding-aling and cat mean, but only obeys when it suits her. She also knows what I mean when I scream, "Will you please sod off, I'm not in the mood for dogs," when she promptly fetches me all her toys, bones, and any socks and slippers she can find, and if that doesn't work drops slugs and snails into my lap until I forgive her.' Sam Coyne, another dog intellectual, a vast General Wolfehound from Oldham, could retrieve golf balls quicker than most players could see them. He collected his own meat from the butcher every day, and knocked the telephone off the hook when it rang and barked down it.

Bobby Walker, the original Half Cocker who looks as though he ought to be lying on silken sheets drinking champagne, and being rung up by girlfriends all day, also suffers from acute telephonitis. As a result his owners have been forced to have their telephone re-sited higher and higher up the wall. Recently they came home to find the receiver on the floor. Later they learnt from a friend that she'd rung up, and been amazed when a dog answered the telephone. Bobby obviously learned this trick by studying his owners.

Mongrels tend to be obsessive people watchers. In my home everywhere I walk three pairs of mongrel eyes follow me, trying to interpret every action; my dogs take in every word I say, picking up a large vocabulary just by listening.

Topsy Thomas, a Jack Russell from Newton Abbot and another acute listener, has picked up fifty words, which by today's educational standards is not bad. They include 'Tiger (the family cat), collar, biscuit, chocolate, cats, paw, Syd, Ben, Nick, Rob, Jacquie and Jane (all members of the family), holiday, maggies (magpies), rabbits, stick, cuppa tea, dinner, bath, bed, box, car, walks, bone, ball, back, sing, no barking, sit, catch, bring it on, drop, postman, liver, dish, brush, see them off, tail, towel, rub down, fire, mat, find.'

Most dogs react to the word 'walk'. In any discussion about

Topsy Thomas

36

Bobby Walker answering the telephone

walking his Bertrand Russell, Many (so called because of the many black splodges on his white coat), Mr Esdaile of Brighton was reduced to referring to 'quadrupedestrian perambulation'.

A lot of dogs also react to the word 'cat'. Bill Fish, a pre-war Bertrand Russell, detested cats in any shape or form. If the word 'cat' was mentioned in any context, he was away with yells and screams down the garden, so the family started to spell the word out, but as soon as the letter 'C' was mentioned, he once again went berserk. Eventually they resorted to the Yorkshire word for cat, 'Fusca', but after a few days only the first letter, 'F', needed to be dropped and away went Bill. Mongrel owners frequently have to communicate by sign language with the dog looking from one to another desperately trying to interpret the signals.

Another mongrel characteristic is resourcefulness. Lady Foster of Sutton, for example, always takes the evening paper to

37

her master when he gets home, but once when he was late she was sweet-talked into taking it to her mistress. When her master arrived she looked in consternation at her mistress reading the paper, then ran to the next room and chose him the morning paper out of the paper rack.

Her mistress often says, 'If you want your dinner, ask your dad.' Whereupon, if Lady barks loudly at him, her master says, 'Don't shout, ask nicely,' and she whines softly. She also fetches cigarette packets and a lighter, and her mistress's shoes, knowing which are for working and which are for best.

Dog observation, perhaps because of their height, is highly concentrated at shoe level. Pinkie La Rue Tyler, a little Collie/Pekinese cross, placed all the family's shoes in pairs in a straight line whenever she found them. (We could have done with her in our house.) Perhaps shoes belonging to different people smell different. Peter Jackson, a white Vertical Shagpile, used to wait for the four members of the family to come home from work; as soon as one appeared at the gate, he would rush to the rack and select the right pair of shoes as they walked up the path, and was there waiting with them in his mouth as the front door was opened.

A great deal of mongrels' intelligence, of course, is employed in furthering their own ends. Mrs Evans was feeling too ill one day to take her Woolly Whitejaw for a walk, and sat down in the drawing-room. Next minute Rusty came trotting in with one walking shoe in his mouth which he laid at her feet.

'I can't go out in only one shoe,' she told him. Two seconds later, he bounded back with the other one.

Dusty Sylvester of Sleaford, a black Rough Diamond, used to demand a new chew stick every night, sitting and begging in front of the drawer in which they were kept. If her owners tried to fob her off with an old one, she would shake her head and give one short bark of 'No'. Del Evans, a black and tan Bertrand Russell, is a squeaky-toy addict. She will rush into any shop which sells them to examine the merchandise, and get up on her hind legs to view the higher shelves before making her final selection. This so enchants the other customers that they invariably pay for the toy. Consequently Del has shelves full at home, and is thinking of starting her own toy shop.

Sappho Steffans, a Black and Tan Tightskin with pixie ears, also knew what she wanted in life. Intensely friendly, she loved sticking her head through the garden gate to be stroked by the local children. One day her master and mistress decided the gate was falling to pieces, and came home with a new wrought-

38

iron one. None of them could understand Sappho's violent disapproval, as she ran around barking furiously.

'She doesn't like the new gate,' said the youngest child suddenly. At which Sappho seemed to nod, put her nose through the new gate, and then rushed enthusiastically back to the old gate which was lying on the lawn. Suddenly everyone realized she couldn't get her head through the new gate, and, feeling slightly foolish, they took dog and gate back to the shop, and asked for one that fitted. The moment they were shown a gate with wider spaced bars, Sappho shoved her head through and barked her approval.

Dog experts claim that intelligence in dogs is a question of serendipity not of reason. This is belied by the times one sees a mongrel work things out. When you drop their lead by mistake most dogs will rush along with their legs apart trying to avoid it, or keep tripping over and nearly breaking their legs. The first time I dropped the lead of Barbara, our junior dog, she fell over and bumped her nose. The second time, she stopped for a minute, thought, then gathered the lead up in her mouth like a bride with a long train and scampered off safely down the road.

Or take the example of Ben Goundrill, a Bertrand Russell, who always alerted the family that he was ready to come in by knocking over the milk bottles beside the back door. Once when he was locked out, without any of the family realizing it because they were all sitting in the drawing-room at the front of the house, he rolled the bottles round to the front, and knocked them over outside the front door.

Ben Goundrill

Mongrels in fact don't make good police dogs, because they think for themselves rather than slavishly following instructions. Texas Rolf, a sleek, jaunty, black, white and brown Prop Forward with huge heavy paws, went with his mistress to the playground one day, where they found a youth with an Alsatian. The youth was sitting on the roundabout as it circled. In one hand he held a ball after which the dog was racing. A good way of giving Texas some exercise, thought Mrs Rolf, getting onto the roundabout and holding out Tex's ball. Texas thought otherwise; he just sat down and waited to grab the ball as it came round.

Tib Brown, an exceptionally intelligent Borderline Collie with a beautiful long face and wise, kindly eyes, used to ride on the roof of her master's lorry. A stickler for punctuality, she always rounded up the family for meals when dinner was ready, and carried her own dinner plate into dinner. Like Texas, however, she believed in conserving energy. One of her tasks was to bring coal up from the cellar for the sitting-room fire. To do this she had to go through the office before she reached the cellar. No one could understand why she was returning with coal so quickly, until they crept up behind her and found she was removing cobs from the office fire which was laid ready for lighting the next day.

Like Tib, Bouncer de Lory, a Romney Marshall, would round up the family at mealtimes, and at bedtime too, if he felt they were staying up too late and ruining his beauty sleep. He also refused to waste time going into the garden to pee, and lifted his leg into his own plastic waste-paper basket in the house. More perhaps as a protest, Pilgrim, Lady Cottesloe's enchanting Corgi Dachshund cross, has also been known to clamber onto the dining-room table and pee on the potted plant in the centre.

Another group of mongrels use their intelligence with an eye to their own creature comforts. When it was cold, Tuffy Hallam, a little Bertrand Russell, would whine at her mistress until the fire was switched on. Rex Wooler-Jennings took matters into his own paws, and despite the fact that he lived in a centrally heated flat, used to claw the switch and put on the fire the moment his owners went out. While Meg Tomlinson, a strawberry blond Rough Diamond, can not only 'switch on electric fires at the socket, but also manoeuvre a pouffe in front to sit on.' Meg can also open every door in the house, especially those of the food cupboards.

In houses with lever handles, it is by no means rare for a tall dog to learn to open doors by leaning on the lever and pushing. Shelley Barton, the mother of my middle dog, Mabel, is a highly intelligent Great Dane/Boxer cross. Having been rescued from the dogs' home, like the dogs mentioned in the previous chapter, she has no intention of ever being separated from her owners again, and soon discovered that doors were meant to be opened in order to get from where you were to where you actually wanted to be. What is unusual in Shelley's case is that she can open doors in either direction. Pushing open is easy, but the clever trick she taught herself was to pull the door open towards her by hooking her front paws round the lever while hopping backwards on her hind legs. Little Glen of Northumberland is not very big, but when he can't see something he gets up on his hind legs and, like Shelley literally hops on both legs.

The mongrel will quickly latch on to the advantages of enlisting sympathy. Meg Tomlinson adopts a limp and asthmatic breathing to gain her own way, then recovers the instant her owners have been panicked into giving in. Prince Hale, a Fox

Meg Tomlinson

40

Terrier/Greyhound cross, broke his paw in an accident. Afterwards it was his chief asset in getting anything he wanted: he would droop it, and wag it around as though it was about to drop off. On the other hand, Rory Patterson, a black-and-white Fox Dog from Leeds, was really in pain with severe toothache on Boxing Day, and kept begging with raised paw to his mouth for help. As no vet was available, his mistress extracted the offending tooth with a pair of pliers. Brave Rory stood perfectly still and even licked his mistress's hand immediately afterwards.

Another aspect of mongrel brightness is their ability to get their owners out of trouble. Mr Cowhig had no sense of smell, but Rip, his Twentieth Century Fox Dog, saved his life on numerous occasions by barking his head off if ever the gas was turned on but unlit. Mrs Gates lost her car keys on a day's outing. Entirely of her own volition, Sally, her Woolly White-jaw, rushed off and barked and barked to tell her mistress she had found the keys in the long grass more than 200 yards away.

Fortunately the mongrel also seems to have an instinct for getting himself out of trouble, often latching on to the one person who can save him. Mrs Dorman of Cornwall sent in the following lovely story from her childhood in Peacehaven.

'One morning we were all woken up by blood-curdling screams. Everyone rushed out of their houses to find a vixen dragging a little Terrier along by the ear. The vixen ran away, and my father, who was a doctor, took the little dog indoors and stitched up his ear. He stayed about a week, then one morning went off and didn't come back until evening when he returned to have his dressing changed. In the morning he went off again, but returned to stay each night and have the dressing changed. We nicknamed him Bed and Breakfast. This ritual went on for another week until his ear was quite healed, and the dressing was left off. He never came back again. But, as a postscript, we did see him playing with some children on the cliffs some weeks later, and he looked very well and happy.'

Perhaps the most remarkable mongrel survivor was Cindy, a small Jack Russell who made the television news when she got trapped in a mine shaft. Miners tried for days to reach her, as did the police, the fire brigade and the local RSPCA. Her pitiful cries grew weaker and weaker, and after much heart searching it was decided the only way to prevent her dying slowly of starvation was to blow her up with dynamite. This was done, and her cries were heard no more. Sadly, her would-be-saviours returned home. Imagine their amazement, several hours later, when Cindy suddenly turned up at her own home, thinner, dirty, but alive and well. The explosion had loosened the rock where she was imprisoned, so she was able to dig through what was left and emerge in a totally different part of the hillside. Fortunately Jack Russells have an excellent bump of locality and she found her way home in no time.

Another mongrel who combined tenacity with a cool head in a crisis was Flash Brooks, a slim, handsome Prop Forward with a sleek white coat. A dog of great character, he sadly died at the age of sixteen, just before this book was finished. Early in his life he lived near an old 30-foot well, which was surrounded by bushes, and only covered with rotting wood. One afternoon he chased a rabbit across the well, and the boards gave way under him. Luckily there were still a few feet of water to break his fall, and although he must have been very frightened he kept on swimming. His mistress rushed off to telephone the fire brigade while his master dropped a ladder down the well, so that Flash was able to hook his front legs over the bottom rungs of the ladder and hang on until the fire brigade arrived. The fireman who carried Flash to safety was rewarded by having a great deal of well water shaken vigorously over him, and his face licked even more enthusiastically. Flash seemed none the worse for the wetting, and was pleased as Punch the next day when a reporter came with a photographer to take his picture.

Like most mongrels, Flash possessed a sense of humour. Jenny Rich, a black Half Cocker, is not averse to pulling her mistress's leg either. 'If I put her out in the garden,' writes Mrs Rich, 'she slips in when I'm not looking, and stands right behind me while I call and call for her. I get really cross and shout, then I feel a little nudge behind me, and there's Jenny looking up with a delighted grin on her face.'

Barbara, our junior dog, like most babies of the family relies on making people laugh to get herself out of trouble. The other day my husband shouted at her for stretching out on his side of the bed. Wiggling like an eel in mock contrition, she jumped off the bed, and seizing Mabel's basket, which is about three times her size, lugged it up onto the bed – naturally on my husband's side – and, settling down in it, pretended to go to sleep.

Finally anyone who has suffered at the hands of sadistic bankers will appreciate the black kamikaze humour of a Jack Russell, called Roo Leete-Hodge, who used to sit on the grass verge and wait for the bank manager's car to come up the drive. Just at the last minute, Roo would walk out and, as the bank manager screeched to a halt, would very, very slowly and with great dignity cross the road.

Flash Brooks

42

Chapter 4

Loyalty

The title of this book came from a very grand, but extremely stupid, woman who lived in Wiltshire. Her husband, whom we'd met at a cricket match, invited us back to his house for a drink. She came home from Evensong, and was understandably none too pleased to find her own Labradors and Springer Spaniels locked away, and her garden swarming with alien children and dogs.

'What breed are they?' she said, looking at my dogs.

'Mongrels,' I said.

She drew back in horror. Then, remembering her manners, she said lamely, 'Well, they're supposed to be *awfully* intelligent and loyal, aren't they?'

Mongrels are probably famous for their loyalty because they realize instinctively that they are less attractive to most people than pedigree dogs, and therefore, like Avis, have to try harder. The stray that has been rescued from the streets or a dogs' home has to try harder still, and is invariably even more devoted and neurotically dependent on his owner. He has known loneliness and extreme deprivation, has loved and lost, and is resolutely determined never to be lost again. Countless mongrel owners who wrote to me described their dogs as shadows who followed them from room to room, even to the loo, and who were reluctant to let them out of sight even for a minute on a walk.

'A dog has one aim in life,' wrote J. R. Ackerley. 'To bestow its heart.'

Once bestowed, it is impossible to measure the extent of this devotion, although the RSPCA tells a nightmarish story of a research student who tried. He cold-bloodedly conducted an experiment in which he gouged out both his dog's eyes, without anaesthetic, and completely lacerated its back, yet found the dog still licked his hand immediately afterwards. Maybe this is a syndrome akin to that of the battered wife who doesn't leave

45

home, because she knows no other master and has nowhere else to go. God knows what syndrome the research student was suffering from.

The most celebrated example of mongrel devotion, of course, is Greyfriars' Bobby, the Romney Marshall owned by a Midlothian farmer called Gray. Every week Gray and Bobby came to Edinburgh on market day, and lunched at a restaurant in Greyfriars called Traill's where Bobby was given a large bun as a special treat. Gray died in 1858 and was buried in Greyfriars churchyard. A few days later, Mr Traill was upset to see an emaciated, starving Bobby slink into the restaurant. On being offered one of his favourite buns, the dog snatched it and bolted. After several such visits, Mr Traill trailed Bobby and found him wolfing the bun on his master's grave. On hearing this, neighbours tried to offer the dog a home, but Bobby always escaped back to the grave, huddling under a tombstone for warmth when the weather became too severe. In the end, he became a national institution. The people of Greyfriars built a shelter near the grave, which he never deserted except to collect his buns, which were the only food he would touch. On such a diet he lived another fourteen years and was buried beside his master.

Less celebrated but in the same determined spirit was the behaviour of Brandy Kelly, a red General Wolfehound, who was rescued as a terrified stray from one of the worst bombed areas in Belfast. When Brandy was very young and still in a highly nervous state, her owner, Mrs Kelly, had to go to the centre of Belfast on urgent family business. Brandy escaped and unbeknownst to her mistress trailed her across several very busy main roads, but just missed the bus. Mrs Kelly had no time to take the dog back, but called out to her to go home. When she returned with a heavy heart by the same bus route, nine hours later, she was amazed and overjoyed to find Brandy, demented with fear, but still patiently waiting at the bus stop.

Mrs Hart of Taunton wrote that she once forgot to bring Trudi, her Old Sea Dog, in from the garden at night. At three in the morning she suddenly woke up with a start, and rushed outside to find Trudi quietly lying in the dark with her front paws crossed in her most-familiar position. Midge Docwra, a white and gold Family Circler, from Kent, was so devoted to her mistress that when Mrs Docwra was away from home for a few days the dog refused to move from the drive, and had to be picked up and carried indoors by her master every night. Even more stoical, was Scamp Wholey, a normally exuberant Rough-

Scamp Wholey

46

and-Reddish, who was left in the kitchen with a dripping tap, and, though his owners did not know it, a blocked sink. Next morning Scamp was discovered sitting in three inches of water, looking very wet and miserable. He had not made a sound all night, although he was an extremely good house dog.

As mongrels are happiest when they are shadowing their owners, it is a great hardship for them to be left in charge of possessions. Battersea Dogs' Home tells a heartbreaking story about a little grey and white Vertical Shagpile who was found guarding an old pair of shoes on a Charing Cross platform during the rush hour. He had obviously been dumped by his master, who'd left him in charge of the shoes, but no one could get near him. In the end a policeman had to catch him with a noose on the end of a pole, and arrived at Battersea holding the dog on a lead with one hand, and the old pair of shoes in the other. Freddie Reid, one of the great *Daily Mirror* photographers, came down to the Home and took pictures of the dog still clinging to his shoes, and reached the pinnacle of his fame when the editor cleared the middle page. English hearts were, as usual, touched, and 700 people wrote in offering Bootsie (as he was now called) a home. In the end he went to live with a hairdresser in Bristol, whose home was over the shop, so Bootsie would never be left alone again. He settled in very happily, was gradually weaned from his shoes and Battersea receives a Christmas card every year from Bootsie and his new mistress.

In his book *In Praise of Dogs*, Daniel Farson tells an infinitely more tragic tale of a mastiff crossbreed belonging to a chimney sweep at the end of the eighteenth century. One day the sweep put his soot bag down in the middle of a narrow back street, and told the dog to guard it. Along came a coal cart, and although the driver swore at the dog, and tried repeatedly to whip it out of the way, the animal refused to budge. Finally, in exasperation, he drove the cart over the poor dog, who preferred to be killed rather than desert his post.

Doris Potter, a portly Satin Crammer from Iver, Buckinghamshire, loves everyone but can't bear to let her mistress out of her sight. Her master and mistress once gave a smart dinner party for some very important Swedish clients. One of their wives couldn't make it to the party, so Doris took her place at table, spending most of dinner leaning heavily on the shoulder of the distinguished Swede on her right. Unfortunately, in her greed, she had positioned herself too close to the table so that when her mistress got up to fetch the pudding, Doris found herself trapped and unable to turn round and jump off the chair. Refus-

Doris Potter

47

Mac Spring

Cindy Slack

ing to be thwarted, she solemnly clambered on to the table and, crashing through glasses, plates, candles and a very elaborate flower arrangement, padded the length of the table out to the kitchen.

It is interesting to find that Spanish Policeman's Hat Ear Dogs are particularly devoted to their owners. Bilbo Price, for example, who has a rough black and tan coat, is never happy away from his mistress, and watches continually for signs that she's going out. He can also read her mind. Even if she hasn't told him she's decided to take him to work that afternoon, he knows and refuses to eat his mid-day snack in case she leaves without him.

An even rougher Policeman's Hat Ear Dog, Mac Spring from Cambridgeshire, is always given one of his favourite 'Bonio' biscuits to cheer him up if he's left behind; but he refuses to touch it until his mistress returns, when he greets her with wild excitement, spitting crumbs out all over her. While a third, Brandy Seymour, who has a smooth brindle coat, goes even further, refusing not only to eat, but to go for a walk with anyone else, while his mistress is away.

Male dogs tend to be more demanding and vociferous in their love than bitches. Fortnum makes an unearthly din when I go out, but I often think his daughter Mabel, yet another Spanish Policeman's Hat Ear Dog, suffers far more in her quiet way. She's only really happy when she's touching me, curling up at the foot of my bed at night, or sitting beside me on the sofa. Cindy Slack, a blond Satin Crammer with envelope flap ears, is another toucher.

'If she's lying on the floor when we walk past,' writes Mrs Slack, 'she stretches out her legs and curls her paw round our ankles holding on quite tightly.'

A darker side to inspiring such devotion is that you feel like a murderer every time you leave your dog behind. In his marvellous book *Jimmy, The Dog In My Life*, Arthur Bryant brilliantly captures the despair of the little brown and white mongrel he took in as a stray:

> A suitcase packed for a journey he might not share, and all the confidence drained out of him like water out of a cup. His tail went down, his head hung, a look of unutterable sadness came into his big brown eyes, even chocolate, which he loved above all else, would remain untouched at his feet if his mistress went out without him. To her, for all his fiery challenge to a world which had tragically misused him, . . . he gave a love as single-hearted and unquestioning as I have ever witnessed in any creature, human or animal.

48

As a result of such owners' guilt, the majority of rescued mongrels are extremely spoilt. My own Fortnum howls if he's left alone in the house, and has now taught his two daughters to howl in unison. This means we can never go out without finding a dog sitter. If I run water for a bath or to wash my hair; if I pick up a comb or a tube of make-up, they start swallowing frantically. The click of the Carmen rollers, or the most whispered telephone call for a minicab sends them slinking into their baskets. Even if I'm simply having a bath and making up because people are coming to dinner, I won't get a wag out of any of the dogs until several people have arrived, and everyone is sitting down to have a drink.

A heartbreaking example of bitch devotion was shown by Jayne Parker, a beautiful Golden Fetcher named after Jayne Mansfield because she was blond and walked with a wiggle. Her loyalty and sweet nature were only equalled by her intelligence. When Mrs Parker went to work, she only had to pat Jayne good-bye, and the dog settled down quite happily. If any of the family were going to be away for a longer period, this too had to be explained to Jayne with much fussing and patting.

One day Mrs Parker had to go into hospital, and in the bustle of leaving and issuing last-minute instructions to the family, she forgot to say good-bye to Jayne. The dog, assuming Mrs Parker had gone to work as usual, went to wait at the front door at six o'clock, and refused to eat or drink or move from the spot. A day or two later, Mrs Parker's daughter Christine, who'd stayed at home especially to look after Jayne, called the vet who gave the dog an injection to dehydrate her so as to encourage her to drink – but to no avail. In the days that followed she refused to touch food or water. With tragic irony, on the day Mrs Parker was due home from hospital Jayne died in Christine's arms.

Perhaps it is because mongrels devote so much attention to human beings that they frequently have human reactions. Peter Warlow of Portsmouth, a splendid black Borderline Collie, was so excited when Mrs Warlow came home after six weeks in hospital that he literally went weak at the knees, his legs refused to carry him towards her, and he could only slither along the floor.

Jayne Parker

There are also examples of dogs actually crying like humans. Andy Rance, a devoted black Half Cocker, hardly moved from his mistress's bedroom door at home while she was away in hospital. When she finally returned, she was safely installed in a chair, and padded with protective cushions to ward off Andy's frantic onslaught. 'It was the only time,' she writes, 'I have actually seen a dog cry real tears.'

49

Mrs Irene Mauldon had a similar experience with Judy, her Golden Fetcher. 'Last September, ' she writes, 'all our family including Judy had a very nasty car crash whilst on holiday. Judy and I had never been parted since she was a puppy. On the day I was discharged from hospital, I expected the usual hysterical welcome, but instead of being knocked off my feet, Judy came slowly towards me, licked my hand, then jumped up beside me on the settee, whimpered and buried her head in my lap, and actually cried real tears. Her face was so wet, I had to dry it with a tissue. I think she remembered the last time she saw me, covered in blood, and thought she'd never see me again.'

Tears, alas, are caused as much by sorrow as by joy. Louise Ritte of London tells a poignant story of her mother's dog, Jacko, a black and tan Bertrand Russell from Battersea Dogs' Home, who was 'purposely chosen because he was the most wretched little bundle.' When Jacko got home he turned out to have distemper.

Jacko Ritte

'He almost died,' writes Mrs Ritte. 'My mother nursed him day and night for a month. He was too ill to lift his head but always raised a hind leg in welcome. When he recovered, we found he was the most appealing dog we had ever owned. My mother and he were deeply devoted, and he always slept on a rug by her bed. After ten years she died, and the day she was taken away we discovered Jacko lying on her bed with tears literally saturating his little cheeks. Ten weeks later, the housekeeper decided to take her afternoon rest on my mother's bed, because her own room was being decorated. This was too much for Jacko. He crept into the room and sitting on his rug lifted his head, and for the first time in his life let out a series of long wailing howls.'

Dogs, like people, need an opportunity to mourn. Whistle Stevens of Launceston in Cornwall, a black Family Circler, always looked after Mrs Stevens' spastic grandson, sitting at the foot of his wheel-chair. When the grandson died, aged twenty-one, Whistle lay about for a week whimpering to herself, but finally sat up and gave a loud howl (the only time she was ever heard to do so) and the mourning period was over.

To end this chapter on a happier note, let us turn to Rex Rees, a black and grey Half Cocker, who had decided his current owner was not worthy of loyalty, and transferred his affections to Mrs Rees, trying to spend all his time in her house. Finally his official owner left the district, taking Rex with him.

'My dogless house seemed bleak and empty,' writes Mrs Rees. 'I sat in the garden, thinking of the splendid walk I would

50

have taken had Rex been around. A dog barked nearby; it sounded like Rex's bark. I ticked myself off for thinking about him too much. Then the bark came again, this time longer and more demanding.'

Mrs Rees ran to the gate and found an overjoyed Rex. Sadly she returned him to his owner that evening. But having found the way, Rex returned again and again, even hitching lifts on buses. Eventually the despairing owner said Mrs Rees could keep him. He went everywhere with her, travelling in cars, trains and boats, settling down everywhere as long as she was with him. In the end, according to Mrs Rees, 'Rex died of old age. We buried him under the apple blossom and something of ourselves died with him.'

Chapter 5

The mongrel comforter

Mongrels are never employed as Guide Dogs for the blind. The 'experts', once again, consider them too individualistic and un-reliable, and claim one cannot predict a mongrel's behaviour in a crisis as one can a Labrador's or an Alsatian's. Judging by the letters that poured in while I was researching this book, this is absolute junk. Not only do mongrels bring comfort and practical help to their owners when they are ill, or suffering from severe depression, but also in many cases save lives by their quick thinking. But then as every schoolboy ought to know, the word 'cur' comes from the Latin 'to cure'.

The great advantage of the mongrel is that being bright, he really uses his brains. Take the example of Sally Gates, a Woolly Whitejaw from Leamington Spa. Once, when her mistress was away, she stayed with some friends who were both old age pensioners. During the night the old man was woken up by frantic barking outside his door. Thinking Sally must want to go out, he got up. Instead, she led him downstairs to the drawing-room where he found his diabetic sister lying unconscious on the floor, having collapsed from an insulin reaction.

Mrs O'Reilly of Sutton Coldfield is crippled with arthritis. On her return from the town one day, her shopping bag got entangled in the sliding seat of her invalid car, trapping her inside. Flash, her Black and Tan Tightskin, tried to help her out by climbing into the car and licking her face. Then, realizing what had happened, he went for help, racing up to a woman miles away on the horizon, and nudging her back towards Mrs O'Reilly's car with his nose. Every so often he would tear back to the car to see if Mrs O'Reilly was all right, then tear back again to the woman, gently taking her hand in his teeth to hurry her along. As she helped disentangle Mrs O'Reilly, Flash 'danced round the pair of them baring his teeth in a smile of pure grati-tude'.

53

'If anything serious happened,' writes Mrs O'Reilly, 'I know Flash would help; it makes me feel safe when I'm on my own.'

Another mongrel of mercy, Dingo Rance, was an unwanted Christmas present. When the Rances gave him a second home, he was, like many unwanted children, extremely naughty, emptying waste-paper baskets and kitchen bins to draw attention to himself. He also stole coat-hangers and shoes to blockade the front door so the family couldn't get in when they returned from shopping. Such delinquency did little to endear Dingo to Great Aunt Rance who also lived in the house. One day, however, she had a bad fall and fainted. Doctor Dingo promptly brought her round by patting and licking her face. After that she became his greatest fan.

Mongrels also display incredible devotion if anyone in the family is ill. Little Toto Cox, a Bertrand Russell, never left his master's side for fourteen weeks after he had had a stroke. Waggles, a black Family Circler with a white shirt-front, also stayed by his mistress's bed during her long illness, and even insisted on having his meals served in her room.

Waggles was very fond of his mistress's friend, Mrs Bowles, who always dropped in on Fridays. One Friday, however, Mrs Bowles arrived feeling very weak and dizzy after having several teeth out, and went upstairs to lie down. This upset Waggles, who proceeded to commute between his mistress and Mrs Bowles, whining and patting their knees with his paw, and pulling at their skirts. Only when his mistress had come upstairs to sit with Mrs Bowles as she lay there did Waggles relax and wag his tail, because he could now keep an eye on both of them.

Mr Mason, a Congregational minister, is also justifiably proud of his yellow Satin Crammer, Lulu, whom he describes as a 'lovely knowing dog'.

'Last August,' he writes, 'my friend Bill had a stroke. While the doctor and I were getting him to bed, Lulu jumped on to the bed beside him. I told her to get down, because Uncle Bill was very poorly. Dr White said, "let her stay". Whereupon Lulu snuggled up to Bill, kissing him on the right side of his face, and patting the other side with her paw. From Friday to the following Thursday, she had nothing to eat, and only left Bill's side to go out. When he sat up for his first breakfast, she edged close, so he could stroke her. I am sure she saved his life.'

After a serious illness, owners often find their mongrels give them the courage to face the outside world. Mrs Welch of North Shields suffered from severe depression and agoraphobia after

Glen Welch

54

one of her family died. Glen, her Black and Tan Tightskin, sensed with true mongrel intuition how terrified she was when, with shaking legs, she forced herself to take him for walks. He kept looking at her, willing her to have courage and more confidence. 'Needless to say,' she writes, 'taking him out cured me.'

Even more altruistic was the behaviour of Dan Lockyer, a Borderline Collie from Broadway. His mistress owned a small-holding and used to sell eggs. One of her customers, Mrs Sargent, detested dogs and, realizing this, Dan always aloofly kept his distance when she called. Then she had a stroke which left her partly paralysed. After months at home she recovered enough to take short walks, and one day popped in on Mrs Lockyer for a cup of tea and a rest, before making the journey home. When she got up to go, Dan left his basket and solemnly accompanied her down the very busy main road, placing himself like a true gentleman between her and the traffic, seeing her safely to her house and returning home again. He did this many times until Mrs Sargent was completely recovered. Only then did he resume his former coolness.

Dan Lockyer

Recent medical surveys have shown that people who own dogs live longer, and are more likely to pull through major illnesses. A dog gives them an interest in life; he wards off loneliness, and the necessity of taking him for walks every day gets the owner out of the house and helps him to meet new people.

Mr Cyril Butcher's wife had had a stroke, and was so distressed when their dog was run over that the doctor advised Mr Butcher to get another dog at once. He went straight to Newbury Sanctuary, and brought home Sandy, a beautiful platinum blond Borderline Collie with a white plumed tail.

'He was a great comfort to my wife during her last illness,' wrote Mr Butcher. 'Since then he has been my constant companion. I live alone in a cottage in a village. Having to take him for walks each day has done much to keep me going and dispel any loneliness. I am now eighty.'

Sandy Butcher

With their sensitivity to people's feelings, mongrels also provide marvellous comfort to the bereaved.

'After losing my husband,' wrote Mrs Winifred Todd, 'and then my son leaving home, I felt so depressed I sat down and cried and cried. Then Tina [a Family Circler] came over and put her paw on my lap, and then another paw on my arm, pulling it down so she could lick my tears away. Then she sat quietly at my side, as much as to say, "You still have me".'

Other owners get over their intense unhappiness by thinking more of the dog's deprivation than their own.

Tina Todd

Ossie Corkery

Midge Cleeves

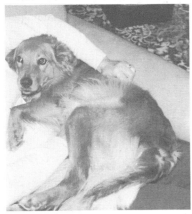

Candy Anderson

'Since the tragic death of my wife,' writes Mr Kielty, 'I have devoted all my time to Patch and I think (?) he has recovered.'

In the same way, after her first child died at three months, Mrs Corkery took on a stray Woolly Whitejaw called Ossie who'd been very cruelly treated, and spent many sleepless nights soothing the dog to sleep. After a few months, Ossie settled down and became one of the family.

'She'll never know what a comfort she was,' writes Mrs Corkery. 'Although she was no substitute for the baby we'd lost, she gave us something to look after. When our first son was born she guarded him like a lion. I remember a friend ringing up at the time. Her first question was, "How's Ossie taking it?" How we laughed when we realized she'd thought of the dog rather than the baby.'

The mongrel can also provide immense practical help to older people. Miss Carus is seventy-eight, and lives with an eighty-two-year-old friend. Walking their dog Laddie gets them out of the house and keeps them fit. In return Laddie keeps the rats and mice down, and once retrieved Miss Carus' canary when it flew off out of the window. Tina Wood, a beautiful Half Cocker, was likewise invaluable when Mrs Wood's mother was ill in bed. She would deliver the paper up and down stairs, and take notes from Mrs Wood to her mother, and vice versa.

Candy Morton, an Alsatian cross, also provides an intercom for her owners. Her master is disabled. If he needs his wife's help, Candy rushes off to fetch her mistress, whining at the bottom of the stairs until she's alerted.

Miss Cleeves of Basildon, on the other hand, is rather deaf. When the telephone rings Midge, her Borderline Collie, barks loudly to attract her attention. Mrs Dickenson has the disadvantage in a crisis of not being on the telephone, but if any of her children are ill and she can't get out, she sellotapes a message to the collar of her mongrel, Samantha, and the dog races round to her mother.

Candy Anderson of Plymouth, a Golden Fetcher, had an even keener sense of responsibility. She was terribly upset when her mistress went into hospital. 'But the night before my op,' writes Mrs Anderson, 'Candy followed my husband into the bedroom (something she never does) and climbed onto my side of the bed. Nothing could shift her. He was so exhausted, he let her stay. When the alarm clock rang in the morning he slept right through, but not Candy, who jumped out of bed, pushed her nose under his arm, and shook him until he woke up. Then she went and woke my daughter. It was as though she realized I

56

wasn't there. After that, she never tried to jump on the bed again.' Even the most obedient mongrel breaks the rules when it's essential.

Finally the prime mongrel comforter must be Bosun Cowhig of Bootle. His mistress has multiple sclerosis and cannot get out. One sunny day in jubilee year when everyone had trooped off to cheer the Queen and Prince Philip, Miss Cowhig was left sitting in the garden, 'tears pricking my eyelids, and feeling very Cinderella-ish.' Suddenly there was a nudge, and Prince Charming appeared in the jaunty form of Bosun, her black Satin Crammer, who sat begging with a red paper rose in his mouth.

'What else could I do,' writes Miss Cowhig, 'but cheer up.'

Chapter 6

Dog Juans

Gladly the cross I'd bear.

Breed dogs, like the ancient aristocracy, have marriages arranged for them. The mongrel marries for love, selecting his quarry on the open market and then fighting off all comers to attain her. For proof of his sexual competence one has only to count the mongrel population in Britain, currently running at well over 3,000,000. Many people quite rightly disapprove of such wrong-side-of-the-blanket coverage, which produces far too many unwanted puppies whose only fate must be the gas chambers of the dogs' home. The Kennel Club, backed by the majority of pedigree owners, would like to see all mongrels spayed or castrated, leaving the world in a few years the sole province of pedigree dogs. The mongrel, however, raises two claws at such Utopian fantasies. Aware that he will never be featured in pedigree dog books, photographed with legs four square, head up, tail stretched out to attract vast stud fees, he is determined to found a dynasty by populating the neighbourhood with his own progeny and wrecking as many pedigrees as possible.

To begin with he scores over the breed dog because he is more available. In despair at the incessant whining and door scratching when a local bitch is on heat, many owners just let their mongrels out (which breed dog owners would never do in case the valuable animal got stolen).

Mongrels are also more persistent. J. R. Ackerley described taking his Alsatian bitch Tulip out for walks when she was on heat: 'A single bark from Tulip would undo us. The locals alerted for news would come flying helter-skelter from all points of the compass ... would desert hearth and home, and, bemused as the rats of Hamelin, staggered, hopped, bounced and skirmished after us.'

Tony Perry-Brown

Tim Harper

If the bitch is kept in, one sees those queues of mongrels outside the house in all weathers, as though they were waiting for tickets for a Wimbledon final or the last night of the Proms. Tony Perry-Brown, a little Bertrand Russell from Cleethorpes, (whose mother, by the way, was called Dick,) was normally a very gregarious dog who went for walks with the neighbours. This routine altered if any of his girlfriends were on heat. One particular bitch lived at the cake shop four streets away. After breakfast Tony would station himself outside the shop, return home for a fleeting lunch, then back again to the shop until evening. He never made any progress with the bitch, but kept up this vigil for years. If his owners walked past and suggested he might come home, he would wag his tail sheepishly, but refuse to budge.

Rebel of Putney, a black Satin Crammer, doesn't even come home for lunch. When one of our local bitches, Misty Lichfield-Irvin, was on heat Rebel sat outside her house from nine in the morning to nine at night for three weeks, and finally lured her out and successfully mounted her in a blackthorn thicket. Misty's owners had been abroad; when they came home they found the garage door and front door totally stripped of paint to a height of five feet, both looking as though they'd been carved up with an axe from Rebel's frantic scrabbling.

The record for door-stepping is possibly held by Tim Harper, a small curly haired, fox-eared Bertrand Russell, who was first found by his present owners outside the pub in pouring rain. The landlord said he had been there for seventy-two hours hoping to seduce the pub Great Dane. The Harpers felt so sorry for this pathetic, drenched love-sick creature that they took him home. Later they discovered he was owned by a local family who disapproved of his rampant sexuality, and were only too happy to hand him over along with his lead, licence (sexual licence as well, perhaps) and several tins of dog food. Although he settled happily into his new home, Tim kept up his sexual activities for seventeen years. Once, when he was nine, he returned home after four days looking like death, pouring with blood and with half an ear hanging off. The vet who stitched him up told Mrs Harper that a mongrel could smell out a bitch fifteen miles away.

On one occasion when Tim was on the rampage for several days he was fed by one of the village shopkeepers. She saw him sitting in the queue at the garden gate, not daring to abandon his post for even a few seconds to scrounge around for a bite to eat or drink, so she gave him enough to keep him going – rather like the coach fuelling the channel swimmer with Bovril.

The mongrel is not just more persistent than the breed dog, he is also more resourceful. Bruce Jackson, a handsome black Satin Crammer, was taken on a three-mile bus ride to the vet. In the waiting room he fell in love with a little mongrel bitch. The next day he escaped from home, and Mrs Jackson only just caught him boarding the same bus for a return visit.

One of the great Dog Juans, Fella Mitchell of Frampton, was rescued from the Bristol Dogs' Home. Lean, raffish, rough-haired with a very shiny nose, merry eyes, a grey moustache and Mephistophelean eyebrows, he obviously oozes sex appeal. According to his mistress he offers his affections to pedigree and mongrel alike and does not believe in class or size distinction. All the local pedigree dog owners try to keep their animals in, but stony limits cannot keep Fella out. On one occasion he pushed his way into a house and scored when the bitch was tied to the kitchen table, on another he jumped off a garage roof at dead of night like Errol Flynn, and mounted his quarry in her own garden where she was being let out for a hasty squat.

Fella Mitchell

An Alsatian bitch in the area was being decorously courted by six suitors waiting outside the front gate. Only Fella managed to wiggle through the gap in the fence, whereupon the Alsatian's owner threatened to shoot him if he broke in again. Undeterred, Fella escaped again next day and headed straight back again. Mrs Mitchell tore after him fearing the worst. Fortunately on the way she was overtaken by one of Fella's human fans, the village postmistress (on a bicycle), who pedalled frantically after him and caught him just in time.

Fella in fact has so much allure that one Cocker Spaniel bitch actually broke into his garden to be serviced. And a local Springer Spaniel bitch, having spent twenty-four hours resisting the fumbling but patrician advances of a selected Springer mate, met Fella the next day and, to her owner's fury, joyously succumbed like Lady Chatterley. It is remarkable how many pedigree dogs prefer a bit of rough trade. J. R. Ackerley's Alsatian, Tulip, was obviously a very highly sexed animal who suffered agonies of frustration whenever she was on heat. When her master tried to mate her with Alsatians she showed no interest; it was only when in despair he let her loose with a mongrel, 'a dirty, disreputable ragamuffin with one brown eye and one pale blue one', that she happily succumbed.

I have had similar experiences with my own dogs. My beautiful English Setter, Maidstone, was wildly oversexed, but ex-

Fortnum Cooper

tremely inept, and would charge across five main roads and ten miles of open country or town to find the object of his desires, only to jump on her from the wrong end.

Fortnum, our senior mongrel, on the other hand, is superb in basket, being a dog of wide experience, deft and efficient. He is also the right shape for a sexual athlete, being compact, thickset and barrel-chested with strong legs that can shift his stocky body at amazing speed when necessary. Physically he couldn't be more unlike the Greyhound or the Saluki, which, as the oldest of breeds are, I suppose, the canine equivalent of the tall, thin etiolated chinless wonder. The great mongrel stud tends to be smooth-haired with a skin that seems too small for his body – like a tart in a tight dress.

The anti-mongrel brigade are always complaining inaccurately that mongrel puppies are the result of irresponsible and indiscriminate coupling. Fortnum, I'm proud to say, has been selectively mated twice in his life, both times to mongrel bitches. On the first occasion we took him to a drinks party in Berkhamsted, where one of the guests said, 'That dog looks just like our Shelley'. Shelley turned out to be a female and on heat, so she was collected in a BMW from ten miles away. The courtship that followed was surprisingly beautiful. Fortnum pranced around with springs in his feet, tail going like a *vivace* metronome. Shelley in her turn kept curtseying down on her elbows, then pirouetting flirtatiously round, then curtseying down on her elbows again and then rushing off to examine her reflection in the fish pond. After a quarter of an hour of such gambolling round the parked cars, consummation took place, with the resident King Charles Spaniel gazing wistfully out of the dining-room window like one of the Lost Boys. The result was five beautiful puppies, one of whom, Mabel, came to live with us.

Fortnum's second mating originated when a friend on the Common sidled up and said could he be mated with her black mongrel bitch, Skip, because he looked such a strong dog. Remembering the joys of the previous coupling, I invited Skip over for the day. But things this time were very different. After a cursory lick round the ears, it was Wham, Bam, Thank you Ma'am, all over in five minutes. After which Fortnum ostentatiously took exhausted refuge on our bed, and growled every time poor Skip approached him. He proceeded to repel her advances until five minutes before she was due to go home, when he got out of bed and, with equal indifference, took her once more. Once again, five enchanting puppies arrived, with the inevitable result that one of them, Barbara, came to live with us.

62

The first mating was obviously a love match, an affaire de cur, and whenever Fortnum meets his first wife they are touchingly pleased to see one another and indulge in endless gambolling. Whenever he meets Skip, however, she no doubt remembers her ghastly experience, and turns on him in a rage. Hell knows no fury like a mongrel summarily serviced.

Mongrels, like people, are obviously attracted to certain types of dog. Shelley, being a Great Dane/Boxer cross – solid, large, short-haired and straight-tailed – was far more Fortnum's type than the just as beautiful but very youthful, long-haired, curly-tailed Skip.

Unlike Fella Mitchell, in fact, Fortnum is not sexually indiscriminate. He chats up most female dogs, but does not necessarily mount them even if they are on heat. Although he is drawn to smooth-haired mongrels and Dalmatians, his real passion is for Labradors, particularly yellow ones. If he meets one on the Common, he'll wrap his front legs firmly round her thickening waist, keeping up on his little back legs, like a wheel-barrow race, as she lumbers after her owner. This predilection probably explains his loathing for male yellow Labradors, because it is they, never he, who are granted legitimate access to Labrador bitches. Fortnum is not the only dog who prefers blonds. Fred Jewell, a slim black and tan Prop Forward from Bedford (so attractive that, when he's locked up, the local bitches queue outside *his* house), also prefers yellow Labradors.

Another pedigree-wrecker was Bruno Vickery, a handsome Prop Forward built on the same stocky lines as Fortnum, but chestnut and white in colour. Owned by the medical officer of health in Eastbourne, Bruno's sexual career was not unlike a doctor and nurse novel. But in his case he seemed to base his selection on owners rather than dogs, always embarrassingly singling out the pedigree dogs belonging to the local medical top brass. His first conquest, a Labrador called Mollie, belonged to the local consultant obstetrician. Mollie had been frequently introduced to chosen Labrador males, but showed no interest.

Bruno Vickery

Bruno bided his time, then one day scaled a ten-foot wall like Young Lochinvar, and was caught with Mollie *in flagrante delicto* by the enraged medic. Fortunately the resulting puppies were so adorable, Bruno's new father-in-law forgave all and even kept one for himself.

Later Bruno scaled another wall and enjoyed the favours of a Jack Russell bitch owned by the senior consultant. He was eventually kicked out with the airy comment that copulation was anatomically impossible. The senior consultant was proved wrong by the subsequent arrival of another large litter, all looking exactly like Bruno.

Joe Lee, a handsome smoky-grey Twentieth Century Fox Dog from Somerset, was equally crafty in his wooing. When his owner's other dog, Sue, a Collie bitch, came on heat she was kept carefully locked up in a loft over the stables, and only taken out in the early mornings and late at night. One evening, instead of following at a distance, Joe crept up into the loft and hid at the back, so that when Mrs Lee put Sue back inside she unknowingly locked the two dogs in together. Next morning when she opened the door, two blissful newly weds emerged – Joe, in particular, looking very smug. The result was three lovely puppies.

Toby Hall, the sexiest dog in Kingston, a sleek black bull of a Borderline Collie, again shaped very much like Fortnum except for his magnificent feathery tail, would hare off at the first opportunity to woo the female of the species, not returning until the early hours of the morning when he would howl on the doorstep to be let in. Laddie Jaques, another Borderline Collie from Southwell, who was rescued as a stray by a policeman and his wife, also used to travel for miles after his girlfriends. Unlike Toby, however, he never came home of his own accord. His owners were always summoned by midnight telephone calls, but couldn't pick him up by car because he was always car-sick. Once, his mistress had to get up at three o'clock in the morning, drive seven miles to collect him, then leave the car and walk him home. (Significantly, Laddie was never sick in police patrol cars when they picked him up. Perhaps he felt some loyalty towards the Force for rescuing him.)

On another amorous outing, Laddie cut his leg so badly that it had to be stitched up beside the road by a vet, who arranged to call at the Jaques' house the next day. When he arrived, Laddie had gone off courting again on three legs.

And here again we come to mongrel stamina and toughness. How many of them stagger home, bleeding, exhausted and dirty, to recover overnight, ready for another assault the next day. It is also a characteristic of the great studs that despite their battle-scarred appearance, they live to a great age. Little Tim Harper is seventeen now. Kim Crook, a Satin Crammer and famous wartime Dog Juan who used to escape through bedroom windows after bitches and only return in a panic when the siren went, lived to eighteen. Bruno died at fifteen, Brutus Collis, a gorgeous black-and-white Rough Diamond with bedroom eyes and Chinese pigtail ears, only died because he

Brutus Collis

was run over by a truck at the age of fourteen on his absent-minded way to see a girlfriend. Charlie Langlands, an Ebony Fetcher with far-seeing brown eyes who used to travel the north of Kent like a sales rep., bringing all his conquests home for tea, lived to fourteen-and-a-half. Kim Hind, a tawny Tightskin, was still pursuing bitches around Sidcup at the age of seventeen.

'He was aware of every bitch in the vicinity,' wrote Mrs Hind, 'and could stand at the garden gate, eyes three-quarters closed, nose lifted and delicately trembling like the tip of an elephant's trunk, as he strove to catch scents borne on the air. This extra-ordinary talent increased his territorial rights to an area of about three square miles.'

Mrs Hind became used to receiving pleading, abusive and often threatening telephone calls which forced her into the humiliating position of having to collect Kim from strangers' doorsteps, and creeping up to the unsuspecting dog on hands and knees in order to avoid a confrontation with the irate owner.

65

It is not just male dogs who are oversexed, either. Many mongrel bitches are equally amorous. Sue Taylor, a Bull Terrier/Alsatian cross, was 'quite the Marilyn Monroe of the dog world', attracting copious suitors and producing a total of fifty-six puppies. In later life, despite being spayed, she managed to breast-feed the cat, while the cat fed her own kittens.

Scatty Weatherill of Gwent, a Spanish Policeman's Hat Ear Dog with a minky-grey coat and great bruised eyes as though she's been on the razzle for days, prefers to hunt for her own suitors, and has already produced at least thirty puppies. Gypsy Kirkpatrick, on the other hand, a Borderline Collie who was insatiable when she was on heat, was no selector of boyfriends. She hurriedly succumbed one day to a white woolly individual who promptly passed on with a sigh like Blake's traveller. Although he loved Gypsy and left her, he did return rather touchingly on the day she produced her puppies, and sat on the doorstep, biting his claws, like any worried father outside the maternity ward.

Some bitches, like dogs, seem to be attracted to certain breeds. Little Heidi Southworth, the original Ear Commodore, hates male Pekes but is irresistibly drawn to Airedales, while Misty Lichfield-Irvin, a Jack Russell, shows a distinct preference for big black sleek dogs. So does Araminta Collins, another Jack Russell from Edinburgh, who hated her pregnancy when she was selectively mated with a Jack Russell, but adored it when she escaped to the illicit embraces of a big black Labrador.

It is touching, too, that mongrels, unlike humans, usually attach very little importance to the dog being taller than the bitch; in fact many bitches seem to prefer small dogs: little Dustbin Hoffmans. My own Mabel, although spayed, has a passion for Jack Russells, and surreptitiously flirts with them every time her pugnacious father is looking the other way. J. R. Ackerley's beautiful Alsatian, Tulip, had a special *tendresse* for a tiny, rather wooden, little mongrel Terrier, with a mean face streaked white and black like a badger. Whenever she appeared, he clung to her hind leg like a limpet (he could reach no higher) while she patiently allowed him to do what he could. Whenever she was on heat, he lived on her doorstep, but between times, when she visited him in the pub in her fond and radiant beauty, he would ascertain there was nothing doing and then rudely ignore her.

Sally Bartle, a Family Circler from Upminster, had the same sad experience. Her only indiscretion occurred early in life with a brief productive *affaire* with the local Lothario, a Borderline

66

Collie. Alas, the romance was short-lived, owing to his fickle nature. Even when she was old, her love for him remained. They used to meet from time to time, and she was touchingly pleased when he took any notice of her – shades of Hermione Gingold and Maurice Chevalier singing, 'I remember it well'.

Not all male mongrels come up to scratch. Errol Roberts, a brindle longish-haired Prop Forward from Walthamstow, when asked to service a neighbour's mongrel bitch totally ignored her and preferred to play with his ball. Described by his master as determinedly homosexual, he obviously subscribes to *Gay Dog News*.

Bobby Booth, a splendidly laid-back Bertrand Russell from Colyton, Devon, also showed marked homosexual tendencies. Known locally as 'the President of the Buggers' Club', he arranged to meet all his male admirers on the village green every day.

Bobby Booth

There are also the mongrel virgins. Buttons Cooper, a lean black Spanish Policeman's Hat Ear Dog, for example, adored her owners but showed no interest in sex at all. While Titty Hurst, a very pretty Standard Magpie who was spayed at five months, has a non-existent sex life except for a strange relationship with her blanket. Like many unmarried ladies Titty has thrown herself into charity work, and visits an old peoples' home up the road every day. She dislikes the advances of all males of whatever species and averts her eyes if her owners undress. Barney Leete-Hodge, a Jack Russell from Devizes, displays a similar modesty towards his owner. He sits on her dressing table when she is in bed, but if she starts getting dressed, he solemnly walks out of the room, coming back later to peer round the door to see if she's decent.

Suzy Evans of Clwyd, on the other hand, a Spanish Policeman's Hat Ear Dog, shows no interest in other dogs but is very forward with her owners, mounting their legs and going for it hell for leather like a dog. Her mistress, Mrs Evans, was a bit worried until she saw the Blue Peter dog doing the same thing on television.

One of Fortnum's great loves in Putney is yet another mongrel virgin, a dog called Emma Ferris (*see* p. 69). She is not spayed but repeatedly repels all male advances, including those of Fortnum, who has courted her assiduously for six years. She hates it, however, if he pays court to anyone else. One day, perhaps to trigger off some reaction, he brought Gypsy Nightingale, one of his many other girlfriends, to call on her. Emma saw them both off in a frenzy of rage, rather like Elizabeth I giving the Earl of Leicester the elbow for dallying with Amy Robsart.

Finally it is nice to know that the age of chivalry is not quite dead. Even though Emma has spurned Fortnum's paw, he still protects her when she is in trouble. One winter night in 1980 she was going for a late night walk through the churchyard with her master, when suddenly two drunks came out of a nearby pub. Seeing Emma in the street lamp light, and envisaging some sport, they moved in yelling and kicking at her with huge bovver boots. Next minute a brindle fury shot from the shadows, and Fortnum hurled himself on the drunks, sinking his teeth into their legs, barking hysterically, and despatching them howling back to the pub. He then escorted Emma and her master back through the churchyard, walking shoulder to shoulder with Emma, and not leaving her side until she was safely back in her own home.

Our family didn't hear about this heroic exploit for forty-eight hours, but when we did Fortnum was slightly bemused, but delighted, to be decorated with a red bow, and given a whole box of Yorkies (the chocolates, not the Terriers, which he no doubt would have preferred).

'I want to be alone': the dog virgin

Chapter 7

Fight the good fight

And so we come to mighty warriors – the Hectors and Lysanders of the mongrel world – who spread ripples of terror every time they put their battle-scarred noses outside the front door. Denied a respectable, even glorious, career as army or police dogs which would enable them to channel their aggression into socially useful activities, they create mayhem in civilian life. As the owner of Fortnum, the most consistently belligerent dog in Putney, I have first-hand experience of this mayhem. Known to his enemies as 'Jaws of Putney', and to his friends as 'the King of the Common', his kingdom extends over our street and the common land beyond. At his approach, young dogs cringe or flee for their lives, while older dogs, attempting to preserve a little dignity, trot off on stiff legs, then break into a gallop as soon as they get to a safe distance. Few local dogs have escaped the wrath of his ivory teeth.

One blessing is that he only hates male dogs. This means that when I go out on the Common, I can only walk with people who own bitches or castrated males, to whom Fortnum also pays court. Every day, therefore, he struts king-like on to the Common with his harem of bitches, which usually includes myself, his two daughters (Mabel and Barbara), two other mongrels, a Border Terrier, two Red Setters, a Great Dane and a Saluki. All of them have to be defended with dragon-like ferocity. If any male dog makes the slightest advance Fortnum wades in for the kill.

He also fights dirty, going straight for the throat. Recently he has employed a deputy in the shape of a handsome castrated Irish Terrier, who acts as official eunuch to the harem. When I, by some miracle, have Fortnum constrained on a lead, or he is engaged elsewhere, the Irish Terrier will send any intruders packing for him.

I have spent many weary hours pondering on the reasons for

this belligerence. They are, I think, threefold: first, Fortnum feels he must protect me from any assailant; secondly, as a result of his dreadful start in life, he is desperately insecure and, like Mohammed Ali, has to show that he's the greatest; and, thirdly, he adores a good scrap.

Over the years these recurrent battles have caused me constant anguish. Perhaps this was why I experienced such a feeling of homecoming when I first read Arthur Bryant's book *Jimmy, The Dog In My Life*. Like Fortnum, Jimmy was rescued from a terrible early life; and he too repaid this kindness by developing into an incorrigible fighter. Arthur Bryant believed that because Jimmy had been taken in, the bond between him and his owners was much stronger than the usual bond between dog and master, and anything that seemed to threaten it struck at the root of his being.

'The fierceness and arrogance of Jimmy's challenge to other dogs,' he wrote, 'I am sure derived from the time when he slunk, a sad and bedraggled little outcast, past farms, the flavour of whose good things was guarded by a proud and angry house dog, and was utterly forbidden to the likes of him.'

Like Fortnum, Jimmy knew no fear, and trailed his coat everywhere. 'He loved fighting dearly, and with any dog larger than himself would engage at the slightest provocation. His mistress hardly dare let him off the lead in the park, and when she did was repeatedly a participant in scenes of the most distressing violence and uproar.'

Like Fortnum too, Jimmy was far more aggressive when out with his mistress than with his master. This was probably because she transmitted more terror at the inevitable reprisals, and he thus felt she was in need of more protection, and also because he knew she wouldn't beat the hell out of him afterwards.

Fortnum never fights when out with my husband and seldom when he goes out on his own. He also behaves much better if I walk him with a friend who runs dog training classes. A commanding bellow from her, and he drops a Yorkshire Terrier like a hot coal and comes careering back to my side.

Arthur Bryant also discovered that fights could be avoided if he totally ignored Jimmy when they met another dog, or called to him sharply at just the psychological moment when he could move away from the other dog without loss of face. Equally, I can sometimes avert a scrap if I leap behind a large tombstone, or the bole of a big tree, so Fortnum can't see me to defend.

The breed dog protagonists would claim that Fortnum fights

72

because he is a mongrel. The pugnacity, they say, with which his unknown sires fought off all contenders in order to mate with his mother and grandmothers must have been inherited by the offspring.

To refute this, I must emphasize that out of the hundreds and hundreds of letters I received from mongrel owners, less than a dozen reported having trouble with dogs that fought, which is surprising when one considers the unhappy start most of them had in life. The common denominator of three of these fighters is certainly the dog's home background. The first is Rusty Harris (*see* p. 70), a splendid Baskervillean hound with a widow's peak pulled down over his forehead like an early channel swimmer's bathing cap, and a very long tail as a result of being tugged away from fights.

'I should have seen the red light when I bought Rusty from Battersea,' said his mistress, 'He was eighteen months, the Dogs' Home wouldn't take a cheque, so Rusty was tied to the wall while I went and borrowed a fiver from a friend. When I came back he was so relieved to see me, he pulled the hook out of the wall.'

Now rising seventeen, he has given Mrs Harris 'fourteen years of purgatory'. Even worse, unlike Fortnum, he is short-sighted and attacks dogs of both sexes, finding it very difficult to tell the difference when some pedigree dog is hurtling towards him. Happily Rusty gets on very well with his non-combative kennel mate, Basil, the original Twentieth Century Fox Dog Mrs Harris rescued from an ABC cinema, where he was dumped when he was a puppy.

Sam Hamilton

Sam Hamilton, a Family Circler with a touch of Alsatian, who died at the age of seventeen, was the second mighty warrior and dogs' home victim. He absolutely adored his mistress, never letting her out of his sight in the house, and howled so badly when she went out that she always had to provide him with a dog sitter. Known as 'the Cary Grant of the dog world', because he looked so young, Sam only picked on dogs his own size or bigger, but lost only two of his innumerable battles – both times with Boxers. After a massive heart attack, from which he re-covered, he went out for a walk three days later and attacked a Labrador.

Pancho Smith

The last of the trio, Pancho Smith, an Ebony Fetcher with a streak of Cocker and Collie, came from the animal shelter at Cheltenham. He was so terrified of human beings that when Mr Smith originally chose him he had to bang the cage to get him out. In a few days he and his master were absolutely devoted to

73

one another, but before long Pancho started to fight. In his case, however, chivalry seemed more the motive than aggression. Once he rescued a little Shetland Sheepdog bitch from the unwelcome advances of a Bedlington Terrier, getting hold of the Bedlington by the scruff of the neck and throwing him all over the place. Over the years, getting Pancho stitched up cost Mr Smith a fortune in vets' bills. The day before Pancho died the vet had made arrangements for him to have stainless steel fangs because all his teeth were broken.

Why, one asks, do owners put up with dogs that cause them so much worry? I would suggest it is the same instinct that often makes a mother love her most difficult and fractious child more than its biddable brothers and sisters. With Fortnum I know exactly how Crippen's mother felt ('He was always a good boy to me m'lord'). For despite his dreadful aberrations, I absolutely dote on him for his brio and unquestionable affection. Fighting dogs are also great characters. Life with Rusty, according to Mrs Harris, is never boring, and he is marvellous and utterly trustworthy with children. Sam Hamilton originally cost his mistress £1. 'His loyalty, tenacity and courage could not be faulted,' she said. 'He was simply the best investment I ever made.' While Mr Smith's relationship with Pancho was clearly the most important one of his life. Tragically, when he was working on a pipeline, excavating a 14-foot trench, the bank caved in and killed Pancho and one of his work-mates.

'Life has never been the same to me,' wrote Mr Smith. 'I buried Pancho on a little hill in Dartmouth, and, as he always slept on my old coat, whenever one of my coats wears out, I lay it on his grave. There lies Pancho, fighter, thief, romancer, daredevil, and for me the missing half of myself.'

Age doesn't seem to wither the fighting mongrel, nor custom stale his 57 varieties. Kimmy Ivey of Putney, a fine Golden Fetcher, is still pitching in merrily in his sixteenth year. Even more remarkable, Kim Crook the second was still roughhousing away when he was eighteen.

Terriers are reputedly contentious dogs, and in pre-war days, when Terriers were at the height of their popularity, there were, as has already been pointed out, more mongrels with Terrier blood, which meant more mongrel fighters. Vets also warn against the crossing of two very popular dogs, Alsatians and Labradors, claiming that the results are often very aggressive. Spaniel and Collie crossings also seem to produce belligerent offspring. We have not only Pancho Smith, but Patch Hill of Cheshire, also the result of a Collie/Spaniel mating. Utterly

Patch Hill

74

enchanting in appearance, Patch adores a good scrap, and on meeting a big dog looking for trouble gets stuck in whatever the opposition. One of the only two adverse letters I got about mongrels came from a Mrs Dorothy Carmadella, who wrote seeking help for her friend who owned yet another Spaniel/Collie cross. Evidently, at the age of two, the dog has reduced its owner to complete despair. 'Not only is he a wicked fighter, but a menace to the neighbours, alarmingly destructive at home, a thief, and a scourge to bitches. It would take a book to report on his rascality.'

Jack Russells, although brimming over with character and guts, tend also to be aggressive. The Don Quixote of the mongrel world must surely be Lucy Hanbury Aggs. Despite her adorably innocent looks, this Cairn/Peke/Jack Russell cross unleashed herself in fury on any dog whatever its size who crossed her path. When coming round from a major operation after tackling a huge Labrador, she sprang from her mistress's arms once more and attacked another huge dog. All her stitches were torn out and it was back to the vet again.

Many dogs only display aggression when defending their own territory. Fortnum seldom fights if he comes away for the weekend with us, and displays most aggression outside his own house. Miss Cowhig of Bootle describes a similar dog in her street called Snowy, who is known locally as the Sheriff. 'Even though he's sixteen now, Snowy leans on any dog who enters his street, and escorts them out. If they go quietly, all is well, but if they put up any opposition it's O.K. Corral time.'

One of the great pre-war mongrel assailants must surely be Pip Taylor, a Prop Forward from Richmond. He had a bulldog head, and a hound body, and would sit outside his house for hours defending his territory. His greatest *bêtes noires* were Jack Russells and the effervescent Airedale from the golf club. Pip also detested a workman called Joe Lee who passed the house every day. One day he barked so loudly that Joe threw his hammer at the dog. Luckily it missed and landed in the path of an oncoming steam-roller, which squashed it flat. Pip was fearless but had no sense of proportion. Once, when a group of elephants went by en route for the circus in Richmond Park, Pip attacked them too.

Pip Taylor

Most mighty warriors have their Achilles' heel. Fortnum has never lost a fight, but has drawn two home fixtures after long and bloody battles. Today when he meets the relevant assailant on the Common, neither party pitches in. They just pass by on poker-legs, eyes straight ahead, without a flicker of recognition.

75

Simba O'Donohue of Inishowen, County Donegal, a Border-line Collie, could hold his own against every dog in the area except one which belonged to the O'Donovans.

'If we passed this dog's house,' writes his mistress, Miss O'Donohue, 'Simba would desert me, and make a wide detour through the fields, meeting up with me 100 yards beyond danger point.' Simba's fighting skills, like Pip Taylor's were often employed against other animals. He always saw off a neighbour's pig when it stole the chickens' food, and once, when trying to evict a stray cat from the garden, he got clawed in the face. Instantly he turned round and reversed into the cat, who was so startled by such behaviour that it fled.

When it comes down to it I suppose I accept Fortnum's behaviour because he is not the first mighty warrior in our family. Rags Whincup, my grandfather's little Rough-and-Reddish, although adored in the parish was the scourge of Bradford where fighting was concerned. His arch enemy was a huge lugubrious hound owned by the local fishmonger called Blackie. Every morning Rags would trot off to see his friend the butcher and collect his daily bone, then try to race home to the safety of the vicarage before Blackie was up and about. If they did meet, Rags instantly protected his bone by standing on it with his hind legs and fending off Blackie ferociously with his teeth and little front paws. Often Blackie won the bout, and would chase Rags home. One day, after Rags had shot panting and boneless into the vicarage, my mother and her two sisters decided to take their revenge on Blackie, and hung out of the window above the front door clutching a large bucket of water.

On hearing Rags break into a frenzy of barking, they assumed Blackie was approaching, and emptied their bucket into the drive. Unfortunately they drenched a visiting curate instead.

76

Chapter 8

The poor man's burglar alarm

Cerberus, having three heads, would not have been accepted by the Kennel Club. He brings us to another aspect of mongrel loyalty – the almost fanatical courage with which he guards both his owner and his property. He will watch as vigilantly over the poor master as the rich, over the old and ugly as the young and beautiful. The story of Jack, a brindle Borderline Collie who belonged to an old tramp called Bill, was told me by Mrs Burchell of Oxford. It is a good example of this vigilance. Bill used to eke out a living by collecting people's rubbish and taking it to the dump; he certainly didn't make enough money to feed Jack properly. The dog always looked half-starved, nor did a matted coat and a wall eye enhance his beauty.

When his horse died, Bill left his shell of a home and moved into a disused caravan, where he and Jack slept on a pile of hay covered with sacks and dirty old coats. One night Jack woke up to find the hay on fire, and Bill still sunk in sleep. Instantly Jack grabbed his master by the coat, and, getting himself badly singed in the process, dragged his not inconsiderable weight out of the caravan door. A passing motorist, seeing the flames, stopped and helped to pull the old man the rest of the way to safety, and then took him to hospital. Jack was taken in by some neighbours. Old Bill was badly burned and only lived for a few days, asking repeatedly for Jack. As a last request the dog was taken into the hospital to say good-bye to him. Soon the newspapers took up the story; Jack got a silver medal for bravery, and the same neighbours gave him a good home, so he was able to live out his life in peace and comfort with his medal on his collar.

The same quick-witted courage was shown by Fly Knowles, a brindle Lurcher bitch, whose stout heart and lovely nature made up for her lack of looks. Her master, Mr Knowles, worked for a crippled farmer. One day one of the farm bulls got loose and, knocking the farmer out of his wheel-chair, pinned him to the ground. Unprompted, brave Fly flew to the rescue, grabbing the huge bull by the tail, and growling frantically to distract him, so that her master and another farm worker could rush in and drag the boss to safety.

Sometimes too the most gentle, timid dog finds unexpected reservoirs of courage in a crisis. Judy Tomlinson, a Persil-washed brown and white Hover Cur with envelope-flap ears, used to chew up the house out of nervousness when left alone. But in Epping Forest once, when her mistress was surprised by a flasher who jumped out from behind a tree, Judy went for him furiously. 'I have yet to see a more frightened man,' writes Mrs Tomlinson, 'running like a bat out of hell with his rain-coat flapping.'

Judy Tomlinson

While Mrs Tomlinson's husband was on night work, Judy used to guard her mistress by sleeping on the rug by the side of her bed instead of in her usual dog chair in the kitchen. As soon as it grew light, sensing that the time of danger was over, Judy would go downstairs to her chair.

Most of the dogs featured on coats of arms are Greyhounds or hunting dogs. In his book *It's a Dog's Life*, Tim Heald draws the reader's attention to the arms of the Phillips family of Stoke D'Abernon Manor, which include resting dexter forepaw on an escutcheon gules charged with a fleur de lys, a dog of very indeterminate breeding. On 4 October 1789, William Phillips, the ancestor of the present Phillips family, fell or was pushed into Portsmouth Harbour, and would undoubtedly have drowned but for the presence of a mongrel dog who leapt into the water and pulled him to safety. Phillips, duly grateful, adopted the dog and gave it proper reward by incorporating it into a coat of arms, where it remains to this day, still looking distinctly out of place surrounded by all that heraldic finery.

The courage of the Dog Phillips was all the more remarkable because he wasn't rescuing his own master, but acting from pure altruism. Prince Hart, a Golden Fetcher and another altruistic mongrel, chased two burglars away from the next-door neighbours' house while they were on holiday. Prince was also well rewarded. When the neighbours came home, they presented him with forty-eight tins of dog food as a reward. Josephine Perry-Brown, yet another selfless mongrel Terrier, dragged herself out of her basket and scared off some burglars when she was in great pain from a kidney disease. Alas, she died ten days later.

Prince Hart

One of the compensations of owning a fighting mongrel, of course, is that they do make wonderful guard dogs. My own

80

layabout, Fortnum, won his spurs the second week after he arrived to live with us by so terrifying two burglars who broke in downstairs that they bolted, leaving all our silver in a sack by the dustbins. He did this single-pawed as Maidstone, our English Setter, slept through the whole hullaballoo, and only got up and barked lustily when the police arrived. Maidstone also ran away when a flasher leapt out at me on the Common.

Mongrels, as has been already pointed out, will repay a hundred times any kindness shown them. Patch, a big black-and-white Rough Diamond, used to belong to a lock-keeper who neglected him to such an extent that the dog spent most of his time wandering round the village. At the advanced age of eleven, the Tyler family adopted Patch, and in return he guarded them like Beth Gelert, even biting the milkman when he stepped on a flower bed. Patch however still remembered his responsibilities to his previous owner, and went up to the village school every day to see the little lock-keeper's daughter home.

Josephine Perry-Brown

Patch lived happily with the Tylers for a further six years, and particularly adored Mrs Tyler because she'd given him such a good home.

'He had a quiet dignity,' writes her husband. 'For some reason I cannot explain, he made me feel awkward and self-conscious when he gazed at me.'

The smaller the mongrel, it seems, the stouter the heart. Rajah Williams, an extremely pretty cross between a Yorkshire Terrier and a Chihuahua, never lets his mistress out of his sight. When out of doors, he is foolhardy enough to protect her from every danger. One day, in Henley-on-Thames, he flew at a Great Dane who looked down at him in complete astonishment.

Rajah Williams

Rajah was not the first brave little dog in Mrs Williams's family. At the turn of the century she writes:

A tiny terrier rushed into my grandparents' hotel and raced round the kitchen barking ferociously and frightening my grandmother and the children who leapt onto chairs to avoid the dog's jaws. My grandfather, hearing the din, came into the kitchen to investigate. He had a way with animals, and as soon as he saw the strange dog, he shouted at it in a thunderous voice, 'Hell-o, Jack.' Instantly the little dog calmed down and fawned around my grandfather's legs.

From then on he became the family pet, frequently accompanying my grandfather to the Albert Hall. When my grandfather entered the auditorium, he placed his cigar on a stone by the entrance, and Jack stood guard over it until he returned several hours later. On one occasion Jack caught a burglar, holding him until the police came, and later picking him out in an identity parade.

81

Jack

It must however be very confusing for dogs. One moment they are praised for savaging burglars and chasing off flashers, the next being beaten for biting the milkman or not welcoming friends.

Biddy Woollard, another endearing little pre-war Terrier cross ended up taking her responsibilities as a guard dog a little too seriously. One day the baker called when the family was out and made the fatal mistake of putting down his basket to pat the friendly little dog wandering round the garden. In no way would Biddy let him pick it up again. He had to wait for the family to return two hours later before he could continue on his rounds.

82

The most innocent and adorable looking Terrier types often turn out to be the most pugnacious. Monty Partridge, a black and tan Hover Cur with snow white paws and dicky, was sitting on his mistress's knee at the vet's when a fat woman with a cat basket started admiring him.

'I wouldn't touch him,' warned Monty's mistress. 'He doesn't like people very much.' Next minute, a large dog was led into the surgery, and predictably little Monty went in for the kill. Having apologized profusely to the owner, Monty's mistress explained to the fat woman and her cat that Monty wasn't wild about dogs. At that moment a bluebottle flew over the other dog's head. Giving a flying leap, Monty devoured it instantly.

'Doesn't like flies much, either,' said the fat woman, retreating to a safe distance.

On another occasion, Mr and Mrs Partridge were having a drink in the bar of the local police station. Suddenly growling came from below. Rushing downstairs, Mr Partridge found Monty dutifully guarding the front door of the police station, while an ashen-faced constable tried to get in.

Monty Partridge

My favourite delinquent of all however was brown and white Mubbs Carruthers, the result of one of the most lethal crossings – that between a Corgi and a Border Terrier. Intelligent and loyal, Mubbs was also extremely vicious.

'So strong was his character,' writes Miss Carruthers, 'he would have defeated even Barbara Woodhouse. He insisted on sleeping in the middle of the road, so all the traffic had to drive round him. He bit with monotonous regularity. We had to pay for many pairs of policemen's trousers. He even bit us if we came too near when he was burying bones.

'He also teased the family horse, nipping its fetlocks. One day he got kicked and was taken unconscious to the vet on precious wartime petrol. But he suddenly recovered en route, so we all went home again. Once when he'd stolen some even more precious wartime sausages, my father was so angry he took Mubbs down to the village fair and offered £1 for anyone who would take him.' (Shades of *The Mayor of Casterbridge*.)

Mubbs Carruthers

Happily that evening Mr Carruthers simmered down and retrieved Mubbs from his new owners, but lost his £1 in the process.

Chapter 9

The street dog

A wandering mongrel I, a thing called Fred or Patch.

Maidstone, our English Setter, was the worst wanderer I have ever met. He could bash his way out of anywhere and cost us over £1,000 in mended fences. Even worse, once he got out he never came home, so we had to bite our nails imagining him stolen by vivisectionists or crushed beneath a lorry, until the telephone rang to say he was watching television or enjoying a turkey dinner in some far-flung council estate. A further fortune was spent retrieving him from various police stations round the metropolis. One of the main reasons we acquired Fortnum was in the hope that Maidstone might wander less if he had a mongrel friend at home. Imagine my horror when, the first day Fortnum arrived, he suddenly vanished. Demented with worry, I combed the garden and the neighbouring streets. I was just telephoning the police to explain that we hadn't had time to fit him with an identity disc, when in he popped through the cat door, meeting me with an excess of amiability.

During that day he disappeared three more times but, unlike Maidstone, always came back within twenty minutes. Later when he grew too fat for the cat door, he would whine to let us know he wanted to go out, then bark to come in on his return. Gradually I realized I had a genuine street dog on my hands.

Like many dogs who've been rescued, he had, in his straying days, roamed the streets, pillaging dustbins when he was hungry, chasing bitches when he felt amorous, and escaping from tight corners when he felt he was going to be run in by the police.

In addition, mongrels tend to belong to working-class owners who are more friendly and sociable, and spend more time in the streets, than the middle and upper classes. If they live in towns they also often let their mongrels out if it's cold or raining, rather than taking them for a walk; thus, even in dogs that aren't rescued, the wanderlust is acquired very young.

One of the salient characteristics of the street dog is early rising. Fortnum goes out on his first excursion about 7.30 a.m. He has lots to do. He must leave his mark on the various lamp posts along the street and round the Common, and check where other canine rivals have staked out their territory before him. It is possible too that the courting couple he saw locked in each others' arms in the churchyard last night might have thrown their Kentucky Fried Chicken bones covered in meat into the privet hedge. The little old man from Number Five might easily have put out some bread for the birds, and Number Twelve, who don't own a dog, had *gigot à la Provençale* the night before last, so it's quite possible the bone has reached their dustbin by now.

On Wednesday, which is the day everyone puts out their dustbins, he stays out much longer on the scrounge, but is always back about eight o'clock to warm his face in front of the bedroom fire and accompany me and his two daughters on our first walk of the day. Around ten thirty, he'll probably nip out again to call on all his girlfriends. If any of them is on heat, he'll check the length of the queue outside her house. If it's too long he'll try and gain admittance later in the day.

Castrating is supposed to stop dogs wandering. It may stop them pursuing bitches, but the dustbin whizzkid carries on scavenging until the day he dies. Otis Price of Putney, a magnificently genial Satin Crammer, controls the street a few roads away from us. He and Fortnum never poach on each other's territories. Insatiably greedy like most dogs with Labrador blood, Otis has an incredible memory for food. If dragged past a spat-out toffee in the road in the morning, he will return on his own in the afternoon to prise it off the tarmac. On one occasion he escaped in Hyde Park, and was found raiding the dustbin of the Hyde Park Hotel by a kindly chauffeur who brought him home to Putney in a Rolls-Royce. His excesses proved too much for him. Next day he was sick on the lawn, regurgitating an up-market medley of haricots verts, asparagus, duchesse potatoes, Tournedos Rossi, and cigar butts.

Arthur Floodgate, a blond Romney Marshall, was dangerously addicted to chicken and turkey carcasses, and had an even more embarrassing habit of eating them over the next-door neighbours' lawn which was cherished like a bowling green. Ozwald, the Floodgates' present dog, has taken the art of dustbin raiding to even higher levels, and only loots food flavoured with garlic and herbs. So persistent is this habit that the Floodgates have had to buy their next-door neighbour a self-locking dustbin.

In these days of sexual equality one is glad to report that bitches are just as good at dustbinning as dogs, Scatty Weatherill of Gwent, for example, a dark grey Spanish Policeman's Hat Ear Dog with bruised bedroom eyes. 'For loyalty, low cunning and intelligence,' writes her mistress, 'Scatty had no equal. We had a house in Kensington and could never keep her in. Friends from Chelsea to Shepherd's Bush would see her crossing main roads at zebra crossings, usually clutching large bones, or Chinese take-away cartons.'

When the Weatherills moved to Wales, it took them some time to realize why Scatty disappeared for two hours every Friday morning. Then they discovered it was the day the nearby village put out their dustbins.

Scatty Weatherill

Other more fastidious mongrels spurn dustbinning in favour of outright theft. Max Cornish, a sleek black Spanish Policeman's Hat Ear Dog, always swipes the next-door dog's food, and brings home his dinner bowl as well. Ben Bell, a splendid Borderline Collie from the Isle of Wight, was an even more accomplished looter. One day he slipped out of the house and returned on subsequent trips with a wool glove, a vast Tory lady's flowered hat, a plastic mixing bowl and a plastic spoon. Perhaps it was a hint about home cooking, because he finally laid a large pineapple at his mistress's feet.

Pancho Smith, the Ebony Fetcher who features prominently in the chapter on fighting mongrels, was also adept at snatching food from other people's tables. During his eventful career he returned home on various occasions with toasted sandwiches, a hot side of beef with the string still on it, a hot breast from a huge turkey, and endless pounds of liver and lights from the butcher.

Mrs Harvey of Cheltenham remembers an incident fifty years ago, when shopkeepers were less obsessed with hygiene, and butchers put meat on wooden benches, or hung it in the open doorway just low enough for passing dogs to give it a good lick. One day Mrs Harvey's dog Nigger, a cross between an Airedale and an Old English Sheepdog, came home with a joint of beef in his mouth.

'Mum managed to hide the meat,' writes Mrs Harvey, 'before the butcher came puffing into the house, but unfortunately there was the tell-tale sawdust in Nigger's long coat, so he was taken out into the yard and given a beating with a walking stick.'

Sandy Shephard, a Rough-and-Reddish of great character,

87

Sandy Shephard

seldom stole food, preferring to charm it out of passers-by, as will be seen in the next chapter. He did once however uproot the vicar's privet bush, and carried it triumphantly home – perhaps he thought it was Palm Sunday. Unfortunately Sandy bit the vicar when the good cleric tried to retrieve it.

The street dog usually has an excellent traffic sense, which is why his owner tends not to worry when he goes out on his daily excursions. Miss Ellen Coath of Southport used to be a governess to a family in Beckenham, and remembers their brown and white Bertrand Russell, Bobby, crossing the road like a human, going halfway, then waiting for the traffic to pass, then continuing to the other side. Scatty of Gwent, as has already been pointed out, always used zebra crossings. Tosca Glover, a black and tan Family Circler, went even further. If the traffic was dense and cars had to stop, she would raise her head to look the driver in the eye, and wave her tail as she crossed in acknowledgement.

Some dogs only wander in towns, where the scavenging potential is so much richer than it is in the country. When she lived in London Suzy Fawcett, a black and tan Family Circler, used to escape every morning, and howled the flat down if anyone tried to keep her in. Fortunately she was always waiting on the doorstep when her mistress came home from work. Eventually she settled happily on a farm in Cumbria where, perhaps because she had miles of space to wander in, she gave up the habit.

Wanderlust is probably partly inherited. Jet Norbury, a magnificent grey Shagpile, had a mother who was an incorrigible escaper. Although her owners have sealed up every hole in the garden fence, Jet, like her mother, still manages to wriggle out every morning for her daily outing.

Jet at least returned home after her outings. But gorgeous George Wing, a grey and white General Wolfehound, never came back of his own volition. Mrs Wing received endless telephone calls from the police, the local station master, and even, on one occasion, from a bus conductor saying he wanted to take the bus back to Kingston but couldn't get George off the top deck. On one occasion, Mrs Wing's daughter went into the bank and found George peacefully sleeping under the counter, probably waiting for a loan. On another, Mrs Wing went out to look for him and eventually discovered him around midnight, locked in the local recreation ground. 'I had to heave him up over the spikes,' she writes. 'His half night inside didn't chasten him at all.'

George Wing

88

One mongrel going by the resplendent name of Geordie Oliphant did however learn his lesson. A compulsive roamer, he once vanished for twenty-four hours. Next morning, when Mrs Oliphant rang the police they said the only people who'd reported finding a dog vaguely answering to Geordie's description had gone off to work, and wouldn't be back until six o'clock.

'I rushed round to their house,' said Mrs Oliphant, 'and discovered Geordie peering out of the kitchen window. He nearly went mad with delight when he saw me, but I told him he'd jolly well got to stay there until six, and serve him right. He never wandered again.'

Wee Laddie Milligan of Glasgow, of the deep brown eyes and pointed chin, was another delinquent. At the first opportunity he would scamper off and chase anything, buses, cars, vans, just to hitch a lift. He was bailed out of every local police station and three times from the dog and cat home. He was always ecstatic when his owners collected him, as though reunion with them had been his only thought all day.

'After he'd scented his way to my parents and my sister-in-law's house,' writes Mrs Milligan, 'he visited them most days. When my first son was born, he went off in a fit of sulks and stayed a whole month with my parents. Despite dire warnings that he would be run over, he died peacefully at sixteen, a dog full of character.'

And this is the problem about the wandering mongrel – like the fighting dog, he is usually, apart from this one aberration, a marvellous character. Caezor Boyes of Newark, a black and tan Ear Commodore, is intensely loyal and affectionate, but once again his longing for adventure is too strong. According to his mistress, they have tried and tried but cannot keep him in, particularly now that he can push the drawing-room window open with his body (having first knocked up the latch with his nose) and jump down eight feet into the street. Before he was castrated he used to stay out all night, but was considerate enough not to wake the Boyes on his return. Instead he slid open the window of the family Mini, jumped inside and slept comfortably on the back seat until morning.

Toby Spice, a young Old Sea Dog, was also a brilliant escapologist who lived a life entirely his own. Every time someone called at the house, he would shoot through their legs out of the front door, or by way of change, would escape through the garden fence, creeping snake-like on his belly until he considered he was at a safe distance, then doing the rounds of the

Ceazor Boyes

89

neighbours' houses and invariably returning with a large bone.

He had all the most maddening habits of the wanderer. He was never at home when his owners wanted to go out. If they drove the car into the country, he would disappear for hours rabbiting. Just when all hope of his return had been given up, he would trot back to the car grinning unconcernedly. Once by way of apology he even presented the family with half a dead rabbit.

Yet as with many wanderers it was as though, by going away, he was proving to himself that his family loved him and would still be there when he came home. In the house he liked to be as close to people as possible, always sitting on their feet, and trying to crawl into their beds at night. Whenever he was made to sleep alone, he ripped up his bed from sheer nervousness.

Some mongrels are such incurable wanderers (why else is Rover such a popular name for a dog?) that they refuse to settle with anyone until they are convinced they've found the right owner. My favourite wandering story came from Mrs Ellen Goodway of Corsham, Wiltshire. Being farmers, she and her husband had many dogs. But the greatest character was a Half Cocker called Peter who had a lovely smile. 'Originally he was the companion of a tramp,' writes Mrs Goodway, 'who wanted to come in from the cold and tried to take lodgings over a fish-and-chip shop. He was thwarted in this attempt by Peter, who spent the first night tearing the sitting-room apart.'

Peter Goodway

Later the Goodways bought Peter for ten shillings in the local pub, and the first night he ripped their conservatory apart. No collar or chain could contain him, but given freedom he proved a friendly and loving dog. At one time he took a fancy to two children who had dropped in, and followed them back home across the fields. But when they tried to keep him he twice jumped through windows to escape.

When Peter had been living with the Goodways for three years they went on holiday, leaving him with Mrs Goodway's brother who tried to take him timber felling. Peter had other ideas however and disappeared into the woods.

About a year later Mr Goodway was driving home to Melksham when he saw an old lady with Peter on a lead. When he asked her how she had come by the dog, she burst into tears and begged to be allowed to keep him. Peter smiled his lovely smile, but gave no indication of recognizing his old master. He had evidently been picked up miles from the woods on the road to Trowbridge, and taken to Bath Dogs' Home where the old lady had chosen him for his lovely smile. His behaviour was so

90

impeccable that she had called him Prince. He slept on a cushion in her bedroom and always had tea in bed. Peter the Tramp had at last come in from the cold.

'I saw him once before we moved,' writes Mrs Goodway. 'He and the old lady were out for a gentle stroll near our house. I made no advances to Peter, but he looked at me and smirked.'

Chapter 10

The sociable Mongrel

Peggy's tail wagged so hard, it hit each side of her body.
Mrs Graham of Anglesey

The anti-dog lobby, having succeeded in getting dogs banned from shops, restaurants and many parks, are now campaigning for legislation to keep them off the streets unless accompanied by an owner. Ideally they would like any dog found loitering to be immediately arrested and clapped in the dog pound. This would be sad, for whilst it is true that the wandering dog can occasionally cause accidents and make a nuisance of himself when a bitch is on heat, there is something ineffably cheering and jaunty about a couple of street dogs out on the toot, or an old mongrel waddling fatly up the road on his daily constitutional.

Mongrels, as Jane Austen in *Emma* realized many years ago, are an integral part of English village life:

> Emma went to the door for her amusement. . . . When her eyes fell on the butcher with his tray, a tidy old woman travelling homewards from the shop with her full basket, two curs quarrelling over a dirty bone, and a string of children round the baker's little bow-window eyeing the gingerbread, she knew she had no reason to complain, and was amused enough still to stand at the door.

The mongrel can also be a sociable animal who cheers people up on his peregrinations. Mrs Hooper, a pensioner, loves dogs but cannot afford to keep one. Fortunately a local cur and his Setter friend pop in to see her every day for a biscuit.

'But not just one biscuit,' writes Mrs Hooper. 'By the time they go my tin looks quite empty, but I don't mind, they give me such pleasure.'

Other mongrels set themselves up as a one-dog welcome committee. 'If Topsy had a special quality about her,' wrote her

93

Topsy Davies

Pippa Woodbridge

master Mr Davies of Oswestry, 'it was friendliness.' One neighbour said that when she came to live in the village, it was Topsy who called on her first and made her feel welcome.

Another sociable mongrel, Sam Johnson, a Basset Hound crossed with an Old English Sheepdog, is the toast of Mortlake, Barnes and East Sheen, with all the locals clamouring to take him for walks. Accompanying him down Sheen High Street is rather like walking with the mayor. From all sides one is hailed with cries of 'Good morning Sam', 'Hullo Sam'.

Bosun Cowhig of Bootle, the Satin Crammer who cheered his mistress up with a red paper rose on jubilee day, loves people but is intelligent enough to distinguish between those who visit for business and those who visit for pleasure. His mistress has multiple sclerosis and when the priest comes every month to give her communion, Bosun greets him gravely before retiring to the kitchen. If the priest visits socially, on the other hand, Bosun gives him a terrific welcome and remains in the room. Nurses are also regarded as 'business', and politely greeted and left. Although he likes visitors, Bosun gets very irritated if they stay too long. He puts his paw on Miss Cowhig's knee with a 'can't you get rid of her' look on his face. Equally, in earlier times, if Miss Cowhig stood talking too long in the street, Rip, her father's mongrel, a Twentieth Century Fox Dog, would pick up his lead and saunter home. Pippa Woodbridge, an adorable little snow-white Bertrand Russell from Dunsfold, will also take matters into her own paws. If visitors keep her mistress up too late at night she will walk into the drawing-room, snap at them, and toss her head towards the door.

On away fixtures, however, Pippa is more flexible. When her mistress's car goes in for a service, Pippa goes too, and spends the day with the garage owner. She often spends days with a friend who runs an antique shop, and whenever she passes the pet shop, she rushes in and does a quick hoovering job. At Christmas she usually gets more presents than her mistress.

Mongrels are often sociable animals because they are owned by working-class families, who tend to be more close-knit and possessive than many middle-class families. Unmarried daughters seldom move away from home. Sons come home for lunch. The men frequently walk to their jobs. Grandmothers look after the children while their daughters go out to work. Uncle Tom and Aunt Florrie still live up the road. As a result the mongrel grows up in and becomes a part of a large extended family.

Mrs Violet Rich evokes a temperament common to many

94

mongrels when she says her black Half Cocker Jenny loves and knows all her three children and all ten grandchildren by name, and would like them all to live under one roof. Many dogs like Prince Sampson, a Satin Crammer from Sidcup, also visit several members of the family in different houses during the day. Prince used to see his mistress off to work at the station, and then stop on the way home to call on her brother and his wife. Susie Dickenson, a shaggy Cairn cross with huge appealing eyes, nearly died when she was a puppy, when she was trapped in a drain. Fortunately she survived, and lived to the great age of seventeen. Exercise obviously kept her fit, because every day she walked seven miles from her home in Lytham St Annes to the Lantern Café in Shadwell which was owned and run by her master, and was where she had her lunch. She also used to call on Mr and Mrs Dickenson's daughter on the way. Towards the end of her life Susie found the return journey a bit of a chore, and cadged a lift home with her master. 'After all,' said Mr Dickenson, 'you couldn't expect a venerable old lady to walk too far in one day.'

Sometimes mongrel friendliness to other people can be rather irritating to their owners. Bitsey Pitt of Chichester, a gorgeous liver and black Spanish Policeman's Hat Ear Dog with a white shirt front and white paws, has the sweetest nature and is devoted to her mistress.

Bitsey Pitt

'But whenever my sister comes to stay,' writes Mrs Pitt, 'Bitsey transfers her allegiance and becomes absolutely obsessed with her, sitting beside her all day and sleeping in her bedroom at night. On the other hand if I and my sister go out for the day, when we come home it is always me Bitsey greets with the biggest welcome.' Greed of course can motivate much sociability. Price Strognell, a fine Ebony Fetcher, used to trot up to Mill Hill every morning to 'visit Miss Og who kept the local garage. In the winter he shared the large fire in her office, and Miss Og would give him a bowl of tea and a chocolate biscuit.'

Tiger, a wandering Rough-and-Reddish, used to drop in on Mrs Henderson for a biscuit and a drink of water, and any scraps, rather like the charwoman in *One-Way Pendulum* who used to come twice a week to eat up the left-overs.

Tony Perry-Brown, the little black-and-white Dog Juan, from Cleethorpes was also very friendly and would lie in front of his house and go shopping with anyone who happened to pass. The shopkeepers all knew him, and had pieces of cake or scraps of meat waiting. He would then return home and lie down until the next neighbour passed.

95

In similar vein, Sandy Shephard of Alton, the splendid Rough-and-Reddish who stole the vicar's privet bush, used to get bored at home and lie disconsolately on the steps watching the world go by. Passing acquaintances usually only produced a wag or so, but one particular woman couldn't resist opening her shopping bag and giving him a sausage whenever she passed. This triggered off a frenzy of wagging, and Sandy would follow her up the street touting for a second helping.

Sandy also adored the local traffic policewoman, who always kept a supply of fruit polos. The children at the crossing used to laugh as he gobbled and cracked them up. If she pretended she hadn't got any on her, Sandy wouldn't budge, but just twisted his head from side to side trying to look appealing, as if to say, 'Don't tease me, I know perfectly well you have.'

George Wing, the Romney Marshall who had to be prised off the top of buses and hoisted out of the local recreation ground, was so popular in the area that his mistress was known as 'Mrs George'. One day when his mistress was taking George for a walk, an old lady stopped and patted him, and said what a nice dog he was. Evidently George had ended up at her party the night before, just wandering in through the front door. Everybody had made a fuss of him, and he had enjoyed all the food but refused to touch alcohol.

Honey Benton, another Romney Marshall of Havant, likes a party too. According to her mistress, 'She must join in the dancing. If no one takes any notice of her, she acts the part of a poorly dog.' At parties everyone also gets a share of Chip Smith, the original Black and Tan Tightskin. He leans on each guest's foot for a few minutes to make them feel welcome, then when he's done the rounds he goes up to sleep on his master's bed.

Some mongrels turn on the charm for gain, but Cindy Waters was more altruistic. A Rough Diamond found abandoned in a doll's pram, there was never a dog according to her mistress 'more admired or popular with all and sundry'. Although Cindy had friends all over the village, she would trot off daily to one particular house, give three short barks, and then be given a sweet biscuit, which she brought straight home and laid at Mrs Waters' feet.

Mongrels even rush in where most dogs fear to tread. When he was on his rounds, socializing, Peter Jarvis of Luton would regularly call on the vet, who would pretend to examine him, give him a pat and a choc drop, and then tell him to go home. Most strange of all, Benny Leete-Hodge, a Jack Russell, was devoted to the woman who kept the local boarding kennels (a place most dogs loathe) in which he stayed whenever his owners went away. He would regularly walk three miles to call on her.

Chapter 11

Diet

One of the great mongrel folk heroes must surely be Good Dog Tray, the Half Cocker who appears in *Struwwelpeter*. In this moral tale we see a sadistic schoolboy called Frederick tearing wings off flies, killing birds, throwing the kitten down the stairs and, most heinous of all, being beastly to servants. He then lays into Good Dog Tray with his whip and boots, until the genial mongrel retaliates, biting Frederick so hard he has to go to bed and take nasty medicine. As a reward, Tray is presented with Frederick's supper.

> But good dog Tray [goes the poem] is happy now;
> He has no time to say 'bow-wow'.
> He seats himself in Frederick's chair,
> And laughs to see the nice things there;
> The soup he swallows, sup by sup,
> And eats the pies and puddings up.

There is a lovely drawing of Tray sitting up at the table, napkin tied under his chin, a half-empty bottle of claret at his elbow.

Most mongrels, it seems, identify with Tray at least in their eating habits. A Spanish Policeman's Hat Ear Dog called Brandy Seymour, for example, eats only what his owners do, including fruit and carrots. Mitzi Jackson, a Woolly Whitejaw who masochistically buries her bones under the cacti in the greenhouse, loves all human food including grapefruit so much that her owners seriously thought of buying her a high chair.

Considering their plebeian station in life, mongrels have surprisingly rarefied tastes. Another Woolly Whitejaw, Bouncer de Lory, refused all tinned food and preferred to share his owners' meals, so they were overcome by wafts of garlic whenever he licked their faces. He also adored smoked oysters and ice cream, preferably together. Nicky Chadwick Rizza, an Ebony Fetcher,

99

also refuses tinned food and loves anything with garlic, particularly garlic sausage. Glen Wilson, a Labrador/Collie cross, even turned up his nose at fillet steak unless it was heavily flavoured with garlic salt. He was always a very healthy dog until his death at sixteen-and-a-half.

Mongrels who are discriminating about their food tend to live to a great age. Rory Patterson, for example, clocked up nineteen healthy years on an almost entirely vegetarian diet. He hated meat and wouldn't touch bones, preferring grapefruit, cheese and chocolate. Sinbad Rowlands loved chocolate and reached twenty-one years by having a bar to himself every night. Peter Ferris, the oldest dog in this book, actually suffered from digestive trouble when he was eighteen months. The vet forbade him to eat dog biscuits or tinned food, prescribing just brown bread and baked breast of lamb. On this simple diet, livened up by an occasional sweet biscuit, Peter, a handsome gold and white Prop Forward, lasted a record twenty-one-and-a-half years, and kept his elegant figure to the day he died.

Blackie Howson of Buxton, Derbyshire (still going strong and enjoying a good bark at seventeen), loves peas, carrots and eggs but will not touch dog biscuits. Bobby Holt (*see* p. 98), now seventeen and without a tooth in his head, is also still leaping round like a two-year-old. Another Woolly Whitejaw, he always has cornflakes for breakfast, but only if they are served in basket in front of the fire. His normal diet consists of chicken breasts or lamb tongues. He tolerates breast of lamb, but reproachfully leaves the fat all round the edge of his bowl. Having been reared on tinned babyfood as a puppy, he refuses to touch anything tinned – even if it's corned beef or stewing steak.

In defence of tinned food it should be added here that little Chip Smith, an incredibly healthy-looking ten-year-old Black and Tan Tightskin, lives exclusively on a diet of Pedigree Chum and dog biscuits. On the one occasion when his master, a cookery writer, tried to inject some variety into Chip's diet by giving him a tin of chicken-flavoured Pedigree Chum, the dog blew it all over the kitchen and wouldn't eat a mouthful.

It is possible that a dog's taste in food may be inherited. Fortnum, my senior dog, wouldn't touch vegetables or fruit, nor will Mabel his daughter, but his second daughter Barbara (by another bitch, Skip) takes after her mother in adoring all vegetables and fruit, particularly blackberries. Simba O'Donaghue, the Borderline Collie from Inishowen, also liked blackberries and would select the largest and ripest ones from the bushes, shutting his eyes to avoid the prickles.

100

Few Labrador owners would deny the insatiable greed of the breed. It seems to follow that mongrels with Labrador blood in their veins also turn out to be extremely interested in food. Fred Richards, for example, a handsome black Satin Crammer, can look very intelligent, but only at meal times. Suzie Buttling of Deeside, another black Satin Crammer, insists on picking apples from the trees when she's hungry. When her mistress tried to cure her of this passion by coating the apples with mustard, Suzie just ate the mustard as well. Before her first trip in a car, Suzie helped herself to some rhubarb in the garden. Not surprisingly, after a few minutes driving, her stomach started to rumble, and she kept pointing out her pain with her paw.

'I tried to rub it without any success,' writes her mistress. 'In the end we bought some Polos. After eating a few, Suzie settled down with her head on my shoulder and went to sleep.'

Mandy Halliday of Edinburgh, a little blond Twentieth Century Fox Dog, had a bizarre passion for potato peelings. According to her owner, she was also 'a terror for grapes; she didn't eat them, but burst them by rolling over on top of them.'

Mongrels in dogs' homes and sanctuaries tend to bolt their food to stop any other dog eating it. Often this habit persists when they go to their new homes. After thirteen years with her present owners, Sandie Woodrow, a beautiful blond Policeman's Hat Ear Dog, still gobbles down her dinner. Another rescued dog, Sandy Williams of Yorkshire who was found wandering in the centre of Middlesborough in 1967, is obviously determined never to go short of food again. A magnificent Golden Fetcher, with a tightly curled feathery tail and the astute appraising eyes of a Northern business man, Sandy guards three houses because they all feed him.

Sandy Williams

'Like all dogs,' writes his owner, 'he has a bottomless stomach. After getting his dinner and the leftovers from our own dinner, he then strolls over to a neighbour's house for another meal.

'Before he returns for the night, he will sit outside a second neighbour's house for his final supper. The owner is a barmaid. When she gets home from work, she goes in the front door, and he walks round to the back. She then makes him an omelette and gives him a piece of cheese. Until three years ago, he was a very active dog. Now his main source of exercise is walking from one house to another.'

Despite his gargantuan intake, Sandy is very fastidious. He likes home-made bread-and-butter, but won't touch sliced bread and margarine. In the same vein, Susie Dolton, a slender

gold and white Prop Forward, loves custard but won't touch it if it's made with powdered milk. While Jet Edge, a handsome grey Shagpile, has a passion for chocolate and rock cakes, but only if they are home-made.

Mongrels appear to be equally idiosyncratic in their drinking habits. Bobby Holt can't get up in the morning until he's had his cup of tea with milk and two teaspoonfuls of sugar. While Sandy Williams, who is fed by three houses, drinks tea with milk and sugar or just milk, but never water. Flash Brooks, a fine white Prop Forward, adored coffee, and if humans were having it would whine until he got his saucerful. At the chink of a tea cup, Bob Follows, a little white Rough Diamond, knocked over his waterbowl to empty it, then picked it up, deposited it in the nearest sympathetic lap and demanded his helping of tea.

My grandmother's grey mongrel, Evans, who was quite long in the leg had the unedifying habit mentioned earlier of drinking out of the lavatory. Tessie Jupp on the other hand refused water out of a tap, insisting on quenching her thirst from the fishpond in the garden.

Table manners seem to be equally varied. Jack King, a marvellous grey and white General Wolfehound, once burnt his mouth on some potato water, and ever afterwards knocked his bread and milk over onto the floor to cool it. To let his mistress know he wanted a drink, Toby Hall of Kingston jumped up repeatedly beside the sink. Robyn Todd, a Black and Tan Tightskin and 'the dearest little bitch in England', bangs her water bowl when she wants a refill (how nice if one could do that with one's glass at drinks parties) and insists on taking thirty-two chews to each mouthful.

Jack King

Sarah Frances, a brindle Edith Sitwell, had a very high IQ. Her master used to give her his cheese rind at dinner every evening. One evening her mistress told her not to eat it all over the carpet. At dinner the very next evening, the moment the cheese and biscuits were put on the table Sarah jumped off her chair and collected a copy of the *Daily Telegraph* which she spread all over the carpet as a table cloth. She then sat on it, waiting for her piece of rind.

Sarah also brought in her own dinner bowl for a second helping, but was never allowed to dine until her master had said grace, and she'd accompanied his 'Thank God for my good dinner' by howling in unison. Eventually, even at picnics, Sarah insisted on howling grace before each meal, even without the human accompaniment.

A great deal of mongrel intellect is concentrated on inveigling food out of strangers. Peggy Graham, a Family Circler, had a passion for ices. At the chime of the Toni-bell van, she would rush out of the house, and proceed to coax two broken cornets filled with vanilla ice out of the van driver. On being given a

Lassie Clare

Pandy Power

third, she would be told to make this one last, and would carry it very carefully back to her garden where she would lie down, holding the cornet in her paws, and lingeringly lick the ice cream.

Lassie Clare, another Family Circler, always accompanied her owners to the local pub. Here she was given a threepenny bit which she held between her front teeth. Putting her paws up on the bar, she would wait to be served a packet of crisps. This process was repeated till her mistress ran out of money, when Lassie would go off to charm the necessary cash out of someone else.

Tiny Lintot, a 'useful mongrel terrier of the highest order', also took matters into her own paws when her mistress was suddenly taken to hospital. Her master was away working and no one remembered to feed Tiny, so she survived for several days by eating turnips she'd dug up from the fields.

Despite their interest in food, however, mongrels are capable of displaying a touching self-control. Mrs Brown of Guildford tells a sweet story about Stacey, her black-and-white Prop Forward, who never stole anything. One day, for a change, Mrs Brown left tea on a low table in the drawing-room. When she came back into the room, she found Stacey sitting with his back to the tray, because he couldn't bear to look.

Other owners are forced to impose self-control on their dogs. Pandy Power, a black and white Shagpile so named because she looked like Chi Chi, is so popular in her village in Wales that everyone gives her titbits. She now has a card attached to her collar saying, 'I am on a diet, please do not feed me.'

Many mongrels unfortunately eat other things besides food and must have constitutions halfway between that of a waste disposal unit and a boa constrictor. Scamp Robinson, reprieved twelve hours before he was due to be put down at a dog's home, developed into a great character as he grew up. His numerous antics included eating eggs and bacon while his master let in the electrician, stealing the Monday lunch of cold salt beef, and eating his mistress's best fur coat.

Simon Brooks, a lovely tan and white Borderline Collie, was another accomplished pilferer. One day a friend brought Mrs Brooks some fish-and-chips for her tea. She left them for a second in order to see her friend out. When she returned the fish had vanished, and Simon was tucked up in his basket pretending to be asleep. Even worse was the occasion when Mrs Brooks had a sore gumboil, and removed her false teeth. Before she could put them in a glass, Simon, presumably fancying a

104

bite to eat, reached up to the draining board, snatched the top set, and whisked off into the garden.

For three days Mrs Brooks searched high and low, and finally went to her dentist for a new set. Next weekend however she was tidying out the garden shed and there, behind the lawn mower, she found her teeth.

Cindy Slack, the blond Satin Crammer who curled her paws so touchingly round her owner's ankles, also did her fair share of destruction as a puppy. She was excellent at stripping wallpaper in her youth and enjoyed eating slippers, and on one expensive occasion even chewed up her mistress's hearing aid.

Dogs tend to eat from boredom or nervousness. Jasper Mc Murray, a Borderline Collie so handsome that one cannot imagine anyone wanting to hurt him, was appallingly maltreated by his previous owners. When he first arrived at his new home he never stole food, but if he was left alone in the house he would chew all the knobs off the washing machine. When left in the car, he also de-knobbed the wireless. Now that he's been allocated two extra godparents who give him a lot of attention, this passion seems to have subsided. Even more dramatically, Bob Follows, a white Rough Diamond, devoured anything metallic – particularly zips and drawing-pins. To his dying day he had a meccano clip fastened round one of his teeth, which seemed to have no ill effects on him.

Coffee Mulvany, a small Golden Fetcher the colour of milky coffee, spent most of her puppyhood in the children's playpen or beside the doll's pram. She loved eating crayons and the numerous plastic toys which littered the house. This dietary supplement, although well masticated, would pass through her system undigested, and a quiet evening walk often revealed what had happened to the baby's rattle or the latest plastic duck.

'Her rainbow droppings,' writes Mrs Mulvany, 'were a wonder to behold.'

My own Barbara has a depressingly voracious appetite. Her father, Fortnum, only occasionally chewed his basket out of nerves, while Mabel only ate biros and the gussets of pants. Barbara devours all before her. She has already consumed forty stuffed toys, three watch-straps, Mozart's Prague symphony, the peak of my ratting cap and the funnel of my hair dryer, and chewed her own basket down to the platform – I suppose she wants to live in a mongrelow. Worse, she has eaten two pairs of my husband's shoes and four pairs of my shoes, so we are now reduced to gum boots and cannot go out in the evening, which is presumably what Barbara wanted in the first place. Every

Simon Brooks

Jasper McMurray

105

Snarler Davoll

time I come out of my study, I find her rising joyfully like Venus out of a sea of foam rubber, with Mabel, her ever sweet-natured sister, cringing in the background trying to take the blame.

But even Barbara's achievements pale beside the devastation caused by Basil Harris (*see facing page*), the original Twentieth Century Fox Dog. Basil, who qualifies for the *Guinness Book of Wreckers*, has already eaten two chesterfields (one leather and one dralon) and three pairs of Charles Jourdain shoes, total value estimated at £2,000.

The King of the devourers, however, must be Snarler Davoll, an anxious-looking Half Cocker with a badger stripe down his forehead. Refusing dog food in favour of all kinds of shoes and duvets, he also offers his abused stomach socks, tights, vast pieces of wood and paper handkerchiefs which he retrieves from the waste-paper basket. He has also consumed a heavy rubber kitchen mat and, at an early age, ate nearly all the fur from his own tail, which has never recovered.

For snacks he enjoys coal, any amount of upholstery or furniture braid, melon skins and old apple cores. In his youth he ate his own leather collar, and with it managed to consume his own identity disc. He has also destroyed the wooden arm of a rocking chair, and devours newspapers with insatiable greed. He can be relied upon to eat the best towel, or chew his mistress's Yves St Laurent tights, just seconds before she is going to put them on.

The situation gets worse if Mr and Mrs Davoll have visitors. In an egocentric frenzy of showing off, Snarler eats anything and everything before their alarmed eyes. Numerous family occasions have been enlivened by his gargantuan feats. One Christmas he ate the Christmas tree, most of it while it was still up, but refused to eat any conventional food, dog or otherwise.

Chapter 12

Mongrel hang-ups

Owners of rescued mongrels are not unlike second wives. They tend to attribute every neurosis or fear to some traumatic event which occurred in the dog's earlier life. Sally Webb, a black, tan and white Tightskin from Hereford, who was rescued from the RSPCA kennels, becomes hysterical at the sight of any man in uniform, and all dogs of either sex. This, her mistress believes, is because she previously belonged to a member of the SAS who, when he was away on missions or whenever Sally was on heat, threw her out on the streets to be the victim of every roving male.

Sheba Ellis was also horribly maltreated before she came to her present home. Although she has settled down well, she is still paralysed with fright at the sight of a tall man or brooms with long handles. Robbie, a big Alsatian cross found collarless and emaciated roaming the streets, has also developed into a calm unneurotic dog – except when his collar is removed. Then, obviously reminded of his previous life, he goes absolutely berserk, shrieking piteously and frantically trying to force his head back into his collar again.

In *Jimmy, The Dog In My Life* Arthur Bryant describes how Jimmy, after living with his master and mistress happily in the country for several years was reduced to a shivering wreck on suddenly hearing the daily bombardment practice from Bovingdon Gunnery for the first time. The little dog became so miserably displaced that the Bryants had to move back to London. Sir Arthur speculates that the sound of the bombardment suddenly reminded Jimmy of the time, before he was adopted by his second owners, when he lived in London during the Blitz, and a direct hit on the house in which he lived robbed him perhaps of all the family he had known and loved.

For a stray dog London during the Blitz must have been not unlike being let loose on Guy Fawkes Night. Even when one

109

bears in mind that a dog's hearing and sensibility to vibration are far more acute than our own, it is still difficult for humans to appreciate the horror to which the stray is subjected by fireworks. Suddenly to hunger, fear, cold and loneliness are added an inexplicable roaring from the skies, the fiendish zip of rising rockets, the ear-splitting bangs, the cascades of burning stars and the cruelly bucking squibs that are so often hurled at a little dog's legs.

By my calculation, Fortnum, our senior dog, must have been running loose on the streets as a very tiny puppy on Guy Fawkes night a few days before he was caught by the gang of louts who strung him up with wire. This might explain his pathological terror of thunder and any kind of firework, even one as innocuous as an indoor sparkler. At the first clap, he dives for the nearest cupboard, scrabbling frantically to dig himself a hole in the floor boards, only to flee seconds later to another cupboard, and then another, and finally to seek trembling and panting refuge in my arms. Ages after the final bangs have faded away he is a shuddering, infinitely pathetic mockery of his normally jaunty, assertive self.

To appreciate the terror a thunderstorm can inspire in a dog, one has only to note the experience of a Family Circler called Blue Quinn. So frightened was she of lightning that one day, when she was alone in the house and a storm broke out, she managed to escape. When she finally crawled home fourteen days later, a shivering shadow of her former self, her black silky coat had turned completely grey.

Patch Wilson

Some mongrels on the other hand seem actually to enjoy bangs. Little Patch Rosgill of Perth always stayed out in his kennel during thunderstorms; he loved the lightning and barked at every clap. While Patch Wilson, a Rough Diamond from Penrith, loved sitting on the lawn watching each flash and trying to catch it. Whiskey Green, a Borderline Collie from Liphook, as well as chasing steam trains and loathing coalmen and postmen, gets quite truculent during thunderstorms, growling at each clap, and then charging through the house each time to see it off at the front door. Some dogs even enjoy fireworks. Bimbo Rawlings, an enchanting grey Shagpile with a sunflower ruff of hair, was a frightful sissy about having his claws cut, but absolutely adored Guy Fawkes Night and was only happy if he went outside with the family to watch the fireworks go off and join in the fun.

Whiskey Green

Other mongrels, like Rupert Pedersen-Hughes, have other hang-ups. Rupert was born in the downstairs lavatory, which is

110

perhaps too close for comfort to the broom cupboard, and passionately disapproves of the plebeian din of the hoover. Tess Blackburn of Brighton, a skewbald Rough Diamond with a Basil Brush tail, hated aeroplanes and barked if they flew over her house, although she ignored them if they flew over anyone else's. Like many dogs she had a love-hate attitude to water. She enjoyed a dip in the sea or the river when it was warm enough, but detested being put in the bath or sprayed by the garden hose, however hot the day. She also hated rain so much that she would often go for more than a day without going out for a pee, if it were raining, much to her mistress's irritation. Shadow Robertson, a vast blond Vertical Shagpile, wasn't mad about water either but during storms would take refuge in the bath.

Rupert Pedersen-Hughes

Dogs, like humans, sometimes hate having their photograph taken. Boris Jones, a black General Wolfehound and failed opera star from Cardiff, is so terrified of the camera that he has to be held by his owners during photographic sessions. Mandy Halliday of Edinburgh, however, was quite the reverse. Understandably vain of her delicate blond looks, she posed whenever a camera appeared, and then barked like mad when the shutter clicked as if to say, 'Thank God that's over.'

Lassie Clare, the Family Circler who paid for her own crisps at the bar was frightened of cars because she'd been in a crash before she came to live with Mr and Mrs Clare. Unable to bear being parted from her new owners, however, she insisted on sitting in the front seat if they went out in the car, but ducked her head below the dashboard as every car approached. When it had passed she would lift her head and lick Mr Clare's hand as if to say, 'Well done, we missed him!' She once saved his life by barking when he was driving too fast near some crossroads.

Patch Hill of Tiverton, a Half Cocker and a mighty warrior of great character, also hates cars. On one occasion his owners were driving down to see their in-laws, and as a great concession they let Patch sit in the front on Mrs Hill's knee. After half an hour he began to heave, a sure sign he was going to be sick. According to Mr Hill, 'My wife said, "Patch, *not* over me." Patch immediately obliged by holding his head over my side, and being sick all down my trousers. Then turned to my wife, wagging his tail like mad as if to say, "I did what you asked".'

It is also fascinating the way a mongrel can pass on a phobia to her offspring. Jan Macnair, a Borderline Collie, was once hit by a golf ball and has since then resolutely refused to put one foot on a golf course. Her mistress now also owns one of Jan's puppies, a very energetic dog called Jill who is always keen for a walk.

Sally Spanswick

Fred Richards

One day Miss Macnair took Jill in her car up to Lyndhurst golf course for a run. Jill jumped out of the car eagerly, but suddenly she sat down and refused to move. Although she is usually a most obedient dog, she just lay by the car shivering. Nothing would shift her. What explanation can there be, except that her mother had told her never to go on the golf course?

Gumboots are generally a welcome sight for dogs. The owner who dons them is usually off on a nice long muddy walk, or at least is not likely to be going anywhere smart which excludes dogs. However, Sally Spanswick of Windsor, another Battersea refugee, seems to have no hang-ups as a result of her stay in the dogs' home except a terror of anyone in gumboots, which of course are uniform for the kennel staff.

Mongrels, being observant, are very conscious of what their owners wear. Jenny Rich, who likes everything to be nice, disapproves of her mistress in a dressing gown. But little Chip Smith, the Black and Tan Tightskin, is perfectly content to snooze the morning away while his master remains in a dressing gown. The moment Mr Smith puts on his trousers, however, all hell breaks loose, and there's no peace until Chip has been taken down to the river for his morning walk.

From a cur's eye view it is easy to see why my own medium-sized Fortnum goes into a frenzy when he sees anyone in a fur coat – he probably mistakes them for a large fierce dog. From a higher vantage point, Moxy Mather of Cheshire displays a similar streak of inverted snobbery. A ravishing General Wolfe-hound, he only allows his equanimity to be upset by the hats at Harrow Speech Day. Mongrels also like a certain decorum. Both Judy, a Golden Fetcher, and Hanna Bool of Kingston are friendly to everyone except men without ties, while Nicky Chadwick Rizza hates dog ends (naturally) and drunken old men at Waterloo.

Among Nicky's 'likes' on the other hand are Guildford and all rivers. Fred Richards loves water, like all Satin Crammers, but detests fishermen – perhaps she had once been ill-treated by one in her youth. More embarrassingly she also detests the colour yellow, and makes a frightful fuss every time she passes a yellow Devon County Council truck – thereby disproving the theory that all dogs are colour-blind.

Many dogs seem frightened of black people – perhaps they sense an antagonism in their white owners. Fred Bartle, the yellow Labrador lover from Chapter 6, goes berserk every time he sees a black face approaching, but he's also petrified of cats and the dark. In areas where few black people live a dog is probably disturbed by the unfamiliarity of dark skin, many dogs, too, being terrified of coalmen or men with dirty faces. One correspondent, Mrs Hazel Wheeler, also remembered an incident from the thirties when her parents owned a village shop in the West Riding. Every Monday the flourmen used to deliver. One morning one of these huge white-faced, floury-eyebrowed creatures scooped the future Mrs Wheeler, then about five years old, into his arms. Prince, her Borderline Collie, leapt to the rescue, grabbing him by the seat of his trousers and hanging on until Hazel's father turned up and managed to persuade the dog that Hazel wasn't in any danger.

Trubble Ward of Gloucester, despite an angelic exterior, detests all traffic wardens. She is also excellent at frightening them off, letting out loud unnerving barks when they approach, whereupon she growls and steams up the car window. Unfortunately she has been known to mistake washing machine maintenance men and nuns for traffic wardens.

Sandy Rogerson, a very phlegmatic dog who slept through the noisiest air-raids during the war, shared the same phobia.

'The only thing which frightened Sandy,' wrote his mistress, 'was a nun so big and black. Although he ran for his life from anyone with a big black umbrella.'

Finally a story to show that mongrels react with their ears as much at their eyes. Fifty years ago Floss Patrick, an Airedale cross, burned her nose very painfully on an old-fashioned flat-iron which had been left to cool. Forever afterwards, if she saw an iron she slunk away. If Mrs Patrick said the word 'iron' Floss became so upset that the family had to stop using the word and said 'Ronnie' instead. Then one day Mrs Patrick was playing with Floss and said, 'I've got my eye on you.' Immediately the poor dog crawled under the table and started to tremble. Then Mrs Patrick realized she had translated the words 'eye on' as 'iron'.

Chapter 13

The mongrel and marriage

If dogs could darn socks and iron shirts I would have married one.

Mr Fish of Huntingdon

The girls at Starcross Secondary School in London are to be congratulated on presenting their departing headmistress, Mrs Frances, with an exceptionally loyal and intelligent leaving present. When she retired early, for family reasons, they gave her a three-month-old brindle puppy called Sara. Supplementary presents included three tins of puppy food, cloths for wiping up puddles, a huge marrow bone, a dog licence, a basket, a blanket embroidered with the school crest, and a navy blue dog coat adorned with an astrakhan collar made by one of the mothers.

Sara, the daughter of a Whippet and A. N. Other, grew up into an enchanting dog who gave Mr and Mrs Frances 'twelve years of sheer bliss'. Training her, as a puppy, must have done

Sara Frances

much to allay those feelings of purposelessness and emptiness that often accompany retirement. Sara also provided a tremendous mutual interest to her owners, keeping them constantly amused with her antics. On one occasion when she had been ticked off for rolling in manure, she rushed upstairs to the bathroom and tried to cover herself with the dregs of Mrs Frances's talcum powder. She loved running errands round the house and would carry clean socks to her master or a duster to her mistress. She was also a great social asset. When invited into a friend's house, she would drag her rug from the car and remain seated on it during the visit. Towards the end of her master's life, she was the only source of fun in the house.

Sara was an excellent example of a mongrel enhancing a marriage. A childless couple can often find solace in a dog. Mrs Wolstenhulme and her husband went out one day to buy bedding

115

Tanya Wolstenhulme

Fly Knowles

plants, and were deflected into the local RSPCA. They were not at all impressed by the only dog for sale, 'a tiny, shivering bedraggled mongrel puppy', and went home empty-handed. Fortunately they felt so guilty later in the day that they went back to get the dog. Re-named Tanya, she developed into a most delightful black and tan Shagpile. 'As we can't have children,' writes Mrs Wolstenhulme, 'Tanya is our little girl. She is drenched in love and we are all happy.'

Mongrels, being acutely sensitive to human emotions, are also excellent at defusing rows. Freda Sandes, a black Romney Marshall found abandoned in a local pub in Manchester, shakes so much when her owners quarrel that they have to stop arguing and comfort her. In similar situations Sandy Shephard, a fine Rough and Reddish, used to fly out of the front door and stand by the front gate, looking suspiciously towards the house to see who was going to turn on him next.

My own Fortnum and Mabel detest rows, and always slink under the nearest piece of furniture if ever they hear raised voices, or anyone ticks them off. Young Barbara, however, is made of sterner stuff, and yells back at my husband with a sort of fluted whine if ever he bawls her out. On one occasion when he and I were having a row he started cataloguing my ineptitudes somewhat vociferously. Instantly Barbara leapt to my rescue, jumping onto my knee and yelling back at him, making us laugh so much that the row was at an end.

In our case, however, the dogs do also cause tension in our marriage. My husband is understandably irritated when they creep under our duvet in the middle of the night, transforming the bed into a hairy gravel pit, nor is he amused when they wake him up by scratching or shaking their ears in creaking baskets at three o'clock in the morning. But at least he and I have always managed to stay in the same bed, unlike Mr and Mrs Knowles who, when they first acquired their brindle Lurcher, Fly, moved into separate bedrooms, Mr Knowles sleeping in the spare-room with Fly so she didn't miss the company of her brothers and sisters. And at least *they* didn't go as far as Doris Day, who had so many dogs that her husband was forced to move into the annexe. When she'd filled up the annexe with more dogs he had to move out altogether.

The RSPCA recently had a similar problem with a wife who turned her beautiful house into a zoo by adopting nine stray mongrels. When her long-suffering husband finally complained, she left home, taking the dogs with her, and squatted in a derelict building in Kensington. The dogs were soon riddled

116

with disease and the RSPCA got permission to evict her and take the dogs to Battersea, whereupon she gave them all the slip and bolted herself into the Ladies lavatory at Victoria with all the dogs. The RSPCA had to smash down the door before they could get them out.

One of the causes of our running battles at home is the allegation that my dogs are out of control and that I overfeed and spoil them dreadfully. It is comforting to find Mr and Mrs Pepys bickering on the same subject three centuries ago:

> At night my wife and I did fall out over the dog being put down in the cellar [runs one diary entry]. Which I had a mind to have done because of his fouling the house, and I would have my will, and so we went to bed and lay all night in a quarrel.

117

Jane and Thomas Carlyle also fought because Thomas was very unkind to their mongrel Nero, teasing him with the fire-tongs, and on one occasion tying a tin can to the poor beast's tail. I hope such lapses were more than compensated for in Nero's eyes by the love Jane lavished on him.

'It is really a comfort,' she wrote after twenty-three loveless years of marriage, 'to have something alive, and cheery and fond of me always there.'

So often unhappiness and loneliness can be lessened by sobbing into the shaggy, solid shoulder of a dog, who provides all possible sympathy but never lectures or gives advice. Sometimes a canine presence can be the one thing that stops a marriage going on the rocks:

'I have been married for thirty-two years to an unromantic man,' wrote one woman to the *Sunday Graphic* in the fifties. 'I find all the love I need in my mongrel dog.'

When the marriage finally breaks up, problems arise over who is to have custody of the dog. One actor friend showed a nice sense of priorities by walking out on his first marriage with a cricket bag and two squash rackets under one arm, and a bag of Spratt's Ovals and the marital Jack Russell under the other.

In a nation of dog lovers like England, divorce judges strongly disapprove of dog snatchers. Back in the fifties the *News Chronicle* reported a cruelty case in which the judge ruled against a husband for taking away his wife's dog, to which she was extremely attached. In summing up, the judge said such an action showed an almost abnormal hatred of the wife.

'A man,' he went on, 'may quarrel with his wife, strike her, but no reasonable man would steal her dog.'

Miss Angela Tober of London considers Snappy, a Black and Tan Tightskin, her best friend, and has no doubts where her loyalties lie.

'If I had to choose between Snappy and my boyfriend,' she writes, 'he would lose. But if we split up I'm sure there'd be a tug of love over her. He's so fond of Snappy he'd probably dognap her if I pushed off.'

Mongrels are sometimes so devoted to their owners that they are jealous when new suitors come along.

'All I can say of Tammy,' says Mrs Rocco di Torrepadula about her beautiful Pied Wagtail, 'is that she would save me from a fate worse than death as she objects to anyone hugging me, so my state of divorced virtue is ensured. Tammy has a lovely nature and a brave heart.'

Rocky Dorman

Snappy Tober

Little Rocky Dorman, a Dachshund cross, was fortunately more sanguine. He comforted Mrs Dorman while she was a widow for seven years, and when she re-married he got on very well with her step-dog, Hannah, who was a Golden Retriever.

Most considerate of all, Meg Stoker, a wonderful Vertical Shagpile with a gleaming blue-black coat and kind eyes, used to try and stop her mistress worrying by removing final reminders from the mat beneath the letter box and hiding them under the dining-room table. When her mistress decided to get married to Simon Stoker, Meg immediately took to Simon's dog, Friday (another mongrel whose card at the vet's ignominiously read 'brown dog'). They both went to the wedding, and accompanied the Stokers on their honeymoon in Scotland.

'She is treated as a member of the family,' concludes Mrs Stoker, 'and shows respect for her position. She is an example to many owners.'

Meg Stoker

119

Chapter 14

The mongrel and children

We had the joy of Rex for eighteen years. He is buried under the apple tree he loved so much. He shared every toy and chocolate with my boys when he was young, cried with me when they were ill, and worried with me in their teenage years.

Mrs Ivy Parker of London

Rex Parker

The anti-dog lobby grows stronger every day. An obscure eye disease which most opticians have never heard of is traced to dogs, and the media go berserk. Dire warnings are issued on television. Bernard Levin and Polly Toynbee leap into print attacking dogs with a ferocity they would deplore in the poor animal itself. MPs press for dogs to be banned from beaches. They are already banned from many parks, which means the places are deserted because people are frightened to walk there alone. The former Director-General of the Health Education Committee weighs in and describes the dog as a 'grubby bag of fur full to the brim with germs'. Even vets have now joined the campaign and warn parents not to allow their children to cuddle their dogs – thus, as Daniel Farson has pointed out, 'sullying one of the most innocent pleasures of growing up.'

As a result, every time I walk down the road with my dogs some hysterical mother snatches up her infant as though I had three mambas on a lead, thereby instilling her terrors permanently into the child. All this is tragic because dogs and children have a natural affinity, and in learning to love and take care of an animal many children learn to love people. My own childhood was constantly enhanced by the companionship of some dog, who would explore the surrounding countryside with me by day, and sprawl across my bed at night, fending off the fears of darkness. My brother and I were always organizing dog shows on the tennis court, and rounding up the local dogs to participate.

One Ilkley matron was most unamused when I banged on her door and asked if I might borrow her mongrel.

'What d'you want him for?' she asked suspiciously.

'We've got a class for the ugliest dog in the show,' I said, not very tactfully. 'We think he'd win hands down, and it would so cheer him up to have a rosette.'

A dog also provides wonderful protection for children, and often has a far greater sense of responsibility than many parents. The orphaned Romulus and Remus, for example, were brought up by a wolf. If Nana, the St Bernard, hadn't been thwarted by the idiotic Mr Darling, she would certainly have saved the Darling children from being kidnapped by Peter Pan. There are plenty of Nanas, too, in the mongrel world. Fred Grimes, for example, a beautiful Rough and Reddish from Welwyn Garden City, always used to wait outside the school to accompany his mistress's children home, and on one occasion saved a little boy from falling into a deep pond by racing across the fields and heading him off until his mother reached him.

A few months later the same little boy, with a group of friends, walked past a shop where Fred was tied up, and stopped to pat him. 'Don't touch that dog,' said the other children in horror.

'That's not a dog,' explained the small boy, 'he's our Fred.'

Price Strognell, an Ebony Fetcher, used to guard Mrs Strognell's baby in her pram like a veteran Gurkha. When the baby was older and had learnt to walk, she suddenly vanished one afternoon.

'Demented with worry,' writes Mrs Strognell, 'I rounded up a posse in minutes. One friend set off down the main road, another looked in a nearby wood, and I myself combed the hayfields in front of the house. Suddenly I saw an upright black tail sticking up like a submerged submarine. It was Price in the waist-high grass, trailing and guarding my witless child.'

Dusty Ireland, a very handsome golden Family Circler, was named after Dusty Springfield because of his black-ringed eyes. When Mrs Ireland's second baby arrived, he took over as security officer, guarding the bedroom door or the pram when it was outside the house or the shops. Pip Martin Royle, a little black Bertrand Russell with fox's ears, also had a strong maternal streak. When her puppies had found homes, she took charge of her mistress's youngest child, turning him over if his nappy needed changing, and allowing nobody but his mother to touch him if he were crying in his pram. While Poodle Loverock, an Ebony Fetcher from Derbyshire, was a godsend to her mistress,

122

always keeping an eye on the children while they were playing in a nearby cul-de-sac. If one of them as much as whimpered, Poodle would start baying like a wolfhound until Mrs Loverock came to investigate.

Sometimes mongrels get almost too protective. Judy Jupp, a Family Circler, always defended the Jupp children when they played with other children:

'She nipped one of my friends who'd made me cry by pinching my doll, and she once bit the boy who was chasing me when we were playing He.'

Another Judy – Judy White, a Dachshund cross with mortarboard ears, also protected her little charges. One day a visiting Poodle snapped at one of the children in the garden. With one leap Judy was at her. In trying to separate them, the Poodle's owner had the distinction of being the only person Judy ever bit. For the rest of the afternoon, until the Poodle went home, Judy positioned herself between it and her children, and from that day black Poodles joined cats as her chief enemies.

Judy White

It is interesting too the way otherwise wayward dogs become the soul of dependability when put in charge of a child. Scatty Weatherill, the Spanish Policeman's Hat Ear Dog, and an incorrigible wanderer, taught her mistress's baby son road sense. Mrs Weatherill used to tie the child's reins to Scatty's collar, and she would never let him cross the road until the coast was clear.

Trixie Hubbard adored going down the playground slide with the children. On one occasion, however, she reached the top of the slide to find one of her charges already halfway down. Sensing the danger, she promptly jumped off the top, winding herself very badly. She never bothered with the slide again.

Dogs are also a great asset to grandparents, particularly those not as agile as they once were in chasing after children. Whenever the family goes to the seaside, Tramp, a Borderline Collie, never lets Mrs Trickey's grandson go out of his depth. He walks in front of the child, gently guiding him back to the shore. Another granny's help, Kim Hurst, a Prop Forward from Middlesbrough, not only guards Mrs Hurst's grandson, but has learnt to rock the pram as well.

Likewise Patch Mills, a Borderline Collie, regularly accompanies the grandchildren to the playground, and cries and worries when they're on the slide, but Patch never takes any notice if he sees other people's much younger children up there.

The mongrel can also, when necessary, be an excellent disciplinarian. During the Second World War, the six Loverock boys persuaded their mother to take in another Patch, who'd been

Patch Mills

left behind by a travelling circus. Patch proved to be a great help to her. Her husband was away fighting, and bringing up six big boys single-handed was no joke, but Patch never allowed any fights. If one boy raised a hand to another, the dog would fly at him. Consequently quarrelling stopped almost overnight. Patch guarded all the family well, and lived to a good age.

Nor do children take long to appreciate the mongrel as the eternal animated waste disposal unit. Anything my children don't like – sprouts, courgettes, liver, mushrooms – is promptly posted down three ever-waiting maws. Time and again I've ordered them to finish up, and, turning round a second later, am confronted by clean plates and a row of innocent faces, occasionally betrayed by a frantically swallowing dog.

Occasionally, however, mongrel altruism misfires. Mrs Samson heard her child crying in her playpen in the garden, but after a few seconds the din stopped. When she went out a quarter of an hour later, she found the little girl playing blissfully with a mud-plastered bone, which Prince, her Satin Crammer, had unearthed from a neighbouring flower-bed and passed to her through the bars.

As well as providing protection for children the mongrel also makes a wonderful playmate. Honey Benton, for example, is brilliant at Cowboys and Indians. When she is shot, she falls to the ground and lies quite still. She plays cricket too, catching the ball, running to the wicket and knocking off the bails with her paw.

Mrs Perry-Brown of Cleethorpes also tells a hilarious tale of how she used to dress up their naughty little Bertrand Russell, Tony, in a doll's bonnet, a knitted coat, mittens on his front paws and bootees on the back, and tuck him up in the doll's pram. One day they were wheeling Tony round the park when he spotted his arch enemy, a brown Terrier called Jack, trotting past and presumably making some *sotto voce* crack about Tony being in drag. Before the children could stop him, Tony had leapt out of the pram and was going at Jack hammer and tongs. No damage was done, but all the passers-by were in stitches at the sight of a dog fight with bootees and mittens flying, and Tony laying about him with his bonnet hanging under his chin.

The little Terrier mongrels, who so enjoy performing in circuses, also have a sense of fun which particularly appeals to children. Teddy Williams, for example, an enchanting pre-war Rough Diamond, lived to the great age of nineteen and, despite losing a leg in a train accident, still joined in all the children's games. When Mrs Williams and her sister were young they

Teddy Williams

124

used to take an old basket wheel-chair up hill and ride down in it like a sledge. Teddy was soon steering the chair down on his own. When he reached the bottom, he would race up to the top of the hill for another go. He also loved skipping with the rope tied to his collar. Later he learnt to hold it in his mouth, standing quite still until it was his turn to skip.

Big dogs are often regarded as better companions for children than small ones because they tend to have more phlegmatic natures. Tiny Rip Wood of Towcester, however, used to help her children build dams across the garden stream, gallantly staggering about with stones twice her size.

Sometimes a dog becomes the communal pet of many children. Laddie, a Borderline Collie, went to school every day at Linskill High School, North Shields. At the end of term he was presented with a certificate by the headmaster commending him for punctuality and good attendance. The whole school cheered as he was led on to the platform. Battersea Dogs' Home also remembers an incident a few years ago, when two very scruffy small boys rolled up at the Home, asking for the immediate return of their mongrel who'd been picked up by the police. They were from the Isle of Dogs, they said, and the dog was a stray – who'd been adopted by their gang of about forty boys, and who slept each night in a different house belonging to a member of the gang. Why had the police nicked the dog, they complained bitterly, when it was minding its own business?

'Why didn't you tell the police it was your dog?' asked the man on the gate.

'We didn't like to say anyfink,' said the scruffier of the two boys, 'because we 'adn't got 'im a licence.'

'But we've 'ad a whip-round and bought one,' said his mate, waving an already dirty and crumpled piece of paper.

Happily the dog soon afterwards turned up at the Home and was joyfully reunited with the gang of forty.

It is perhaps during adolescence that the mongrel can be of most comfort, welcoming and guarding the latch-key child when both parents are out at work, and going a long way to assuage that isolation and loneliness that many teenagers feel.

Fred Clayton Smith of Offerton, born in 1916, still remembers how his miserably unhappy childhood was redeemed by the companionship of Queenie, a big rough-coated bitch, whom he rescued from drowning in the river. He took her home, despite the protests of his drunken father who detested dogs, and made her a snug kennel out of a beer barrel filled with straw; and earned enough money for her keep by running errands for the butcher.

'Thus began,' writes Mr Smith, 'the most wonderful relationship I had as a small boy. Queenie was the most loyal creature I've ever met, flying at my father when he raised his fist at me. When he was drunk, I used to hide in her kennel. Together we roamed the fields, and I helped her to conquer her fear of water. She learnt to bring in the cows without running them, and always went with me on my milk round in the morning. When I started work, she came to see me off. One morning she didn't come when I called. I found her dead in her kennel, still curled up and warm. I carried her gently into the churchyard and buried her under the copper beech in the corner. She was more worthy to be there than many who'd been buried there before her with so much pomp and ceremony.'

A heartbreaking letter also came from a little girl from Ormskirk called Carol, who befriended a neighbour's Ear Commodore, and took her for walks every day. One day, however, she arrived to collect the dog and found the owners had had her put down. Carol was inconsolable, crying herself to sleep for weeks afterwards.

'Never,' she wrote, 'have I had such a true loving friend. I am writing to you in the hope that you will understand how I felt, and realize I can never put into words how wonderful she really was. You could never mistake Zoie for another dog, because she had one floppy ear which made her even more lovely.'

Another teenager, David Bellett of Stepney, was going through the typically rebellious adolescent stage of running away from home, and being repeatedly suspended from his grammar school. After a major row with his parents, he packed a rucksack and, with £12 in his pocket, headed for Battersea, because he'd always wanted a dog. He emerged from the Home half an hour later having acquired a fellow adolescent: a huge but emaciated sandy mongrel, who'd come up to the bars and licked his hand. He named the dog Rebel. It had cost him, including collar and lead, £11.50. Together they trekked to Roehampton, where David's last 50p went on a bottle of pop and a packet of crisps which Rebel shared. The dog was obviously ravenous, but never once during the long day did he growl or grumble, but just kept walking close to David's side, occasionally licking his hand to reassure him. By one o'clock in the morning they were both exhausted, and decided to bed down under a tree. 'Feeling this big friendly animal by my side,' writes David, 'I started wondering how I was going to feed him, then I

Zoie

127

thought of my parents and how worried they must be, went straight to a telephone box, and rang home. I told them I'd got a big dog. They were so relieved they wouldn't have minded an elephant. My father came and picked us up, and fell in love with Rebel at once.'

Rebel's troubles however were not over. Next day it was plain that he had distemper. He nearly died. The entire Bellett family joined forces to save his life, nursing him all round the clock. Happily he pulled through. After such communal achievement, David patched up his differences with his parents, and is now happily working as a French polisher.

One man who never underestimates the bond between a child and his dog is Fred Winterflood BEM who has been associated with Battersea Dogs' Home for forty years, but has always retained his sense of humour and compassion. One morning he was manning the reception desk when a little red nose appeared over the counter.

'Please mister,' whispered a very small boy, 'I've lost my dog.'

His father, who followed him, said they'd spent the two previous days and nights searching for the dog, an old mongrel who'd grown up with the boy. The child had insisted on leaving his bedroom light on all night to guide the dog home, and was desperately worried because the animal usually slept on his bed. How would he ever get to sleep at night if he didn't have a bed to lie on?

Although the father took several weeks off work to help in the search, and the child checked in to the dogs' home every day, no old mongrel turned up. But the heart of Battersea (hardened so often only out of necessity) was touched by the small boy's desolation. They offered him any dog in the home (including two magnificent St Bernards resident at the time) free of charge to replace his lost pet. He shook his head – he only wanted his old dog.

So Battersea went even further, and had a photograph of the dog blown up and pinned over the door where all stray dogs are checked in on arrival – just in case any of them matched up. Twelve weeks dragged by, then a particular keeper, remarkable in his skill at recognizing dogs, reported to the general office that he thought he'd found the dog – a pitifully thin brown and black mongrel.

Mr Winterflood looked at the animal in question and scoffed. The creature was a completely different size, he said.

'Look at the markings on the back,' said the keeper. 'Remem-

128

ber he's been missing the boy, and probably on the run, for weeks.'

With little feeling of optimism, Mr Winterflood rang up the boy's mother, warning her not to tell the child in case it wasn't the right dog, but just to pop in on a routine visit.

The little dog was tethered to the bars. It waited unkempt, dead-eyed, unsteady on its legs, the picture of dejection. But as soon as the little boy shuffled slowly down the line, listlessly examining each dog, it pricked its ears, stared for a second, whimpered unbelievingly, then went absolutely crazy with excitement. The little boy was speechless. He just staggered forward and cuddled the dog incredulously as it frantically licked away the tears of joy which streaked his face. So delighted were the staff of Battersea by the reunion that, as a final gesture, they had a whip round and brought the dog a new collar and lead.

Chapter 15

Non-pedigree chums

The mongrel is often as touchingly loyal to other dogs as he is to his master. Rags, my grandfather's little Rough and Reddish, for example, was very fond of his father, who lived on a farm up the valley. Every day he wriggled his way through the garden fence, and scampered off to visit him. While Bosun Cowhig of Bootle, the Satin Crammer, was devoted both to his mother and his brother. Whenever he met them in the street he greeted them rapturously. If they turned up at his house, he insisted on sharing his dinner with them, taking a few bites himself, then standing back and wagging his tail in the best *maître d'hôtel* fashion while his mother and brother finished up.

Another remarkable instance of unselfishness was shown by Micky Keay, a black Satin Crammer with a white chest, from Liverpool. In 1968 he suddenly went off his food and started losing weight dramatically. He wouldn't touch his dinner, but if offered biscuits or cakes would snatch them up and rush out into the garden, returning a few minutes later begging for more. He got so thin that his mistress took him to the vet, who could only suggest that he was fretting for his master who'd died earlier in the year. One day, however, Mrs Keay solved the problem by coming home unexpectedly and finding an emaciated, sickly-looking blond Satin Crammer wolfing Micky's dinner in the kitchen while Micky kept guard. Mrs Keay then followed Micky when he went outside with his next piece of cake, and sure enough found him giving it to the poor bitch who was cowering in the potting shed at the bottom of the garden. When no one claimed her, Mrs Keay took the bitch in and called her Sally; and for twelve years the two dogs were inseparable, until poor Micky died of rat poison in July 1980.

Instantly, the heartbroken Sally stopped eating, and literally fretted herself to death. As a last resort the vet suggested getting a tiny puppy to shake Sally out of her despondency. It didn't

Sally and Micky Keay

Brandy and Samba Baker-Beale

work. Sally lingered on for only a week after the new puppy arrived, but heroically the night before she died she struggled out of her basket and painstakingly taught the tiny thing to lap from a saucer, and by spreading her claws out and licking between them, showed him how to clean his little paws.

Samba Baker-Beale, a Pied Wagtail with pointed ears from Bognor Regis, was obviously like Micky Kaey, longing for a friend so much that she brought home one stray dog after another for her mistress to inspect. Finally she turned up with Brandy, a yellow Satin Crammer who'd been appallingly mal-treated. Samba's owner adopted Brandy, and Samba absolutely dotes on him, 'giving him everything except her food, as one can see by her figure.'

Devotion, of course, tends to be more unclouded if the dog, not the owner, is the one who initiates the friendship, mongrels preferring to choose their own mates rather than have new ones thrust upon them. When Mabel, Fortnum's daughter, came to live with us we had two months of deep sulks, growls and curling lips from Fortnum, until Mabel learnt her place and stopped trying to endear herself to him. When in her turn Barbara, Fortnum's second daughter arrived, we got deep sulks, curling lips and sighs from Mabel. Being a much nicer-natured dog than her father, she put up with Barbara's rough-housing and puppyish presumption, but always with an expression of martyrdom on her face. She made it clear to all of us what a terrible time she was having. They have now all learnt to tolerate each other, and although they snap occasionally, each will defend the others against a common foe.

Most dogs, in fact, overcome their jealousy in a crisis. Prince Trickey, a Pied Wagtail, was absolutely livid when Tramp, a smooth Borderline Collie, joined the Trickey household. But when Tramp vanished for twenty-four hours on his first taste of courtship, Prince refused to eat until he returned.

In his book *In Praise of Dogs*, Daniel Farson also tells the true story of Fan, the bad-tempered mongrel Terrier who always slept on a special shawl on her mistress's bed and growled if anyone approached. Her venom was particularly reserved for her mistress's other dog, a charming Bull Terrier called Rose. One day, however, Rose spiked herself jumping over a fence, and spent ten days at the vet's fighting for her life. On her return, the normally cantankerous Fan greeted Rose with ecstasy, and didn't even snap when the young Bulldog, over-whelmed by such a reception, rushed upstairs and collapsed on the sacred shawl in a rapture of relief. To everyone's amaze-

132

ment, Fan licked Rose that night as though she was her own lost puppy, then turned stoically away, leaving her in possession of the shawl, and curled up at the foot of the bed. Next day, she allowed Rose to sleep beside her on the shawl, but the following day, realizing Rose had recovered, sympathy evaporated. Snappily banishing Rose, Fan took sole possession of the shawl once more.

When a mongrel moves into a house with a pedigree dog, as has already been pointed out, it takes over. Winston, a Springer Spaniel (despite being twice the size of Bobby his mongrel kennel mate and able to gobble him up with one mouthful) always toes the line when Bobby is around. A low throaty growl from Bobby sends him shivering behind the sofa.

When Fortnum came to live with us, he immediately made friends with our Setter, Maidstone, following him round the house and hanging on his every bark. But after a week of sycophancy, Fortnum's natural bossiness asserted itself. He started ticking Maidstone off if he stepped out of line, biting his ankles on the Common if he didn't return when I called him. He even attempted to smarten the unkempt Maidstone up, cleaning his ears, teeth, and eyes every morning, and chuntering over his toilet like an ancient valet.

When a group of mongrels live in a house together, one finds the most intelligent one usually outsmarts the others. Fortnum and Barbara are far more assertive than Mabel and invariably bag the best seats, on either side of me, on the sofa. Whereupon Mabel waits reproachfully for a few minutes, then goes to the door and gives a terrific bark, sending the other two racing out to the front door. Mabel then nips back, and occupies one of the best places beside me.

Susie Bill of Harlow, a red Fetcher, also used to outsmart her kennel mate, a black Satin Crammer called Ben. When he was hogging the fire, she would pretend that she wanted to go out. The moment Ben followed her to the back door, she'd do a U turn back into the drawing-room and monopolize the fire.

Brandy and Sherry Holden are the gold and white Rough Diamond offspring of a Wirehaired Terrier/Shetland Sheepdog crossing. Although they are alike in looks, only Brandy inherited the Terrier cunning. She wolfs her dinner, emptying her bowl first, then leaps adoringly onto her mistress's lap, knowing this will make Sherry so jealous that she will leave her food and rush over to her mistress. Whereupon Brandy leaps down, and polishes off Sherry's leftovers.

Despite such jealousy, one is constantly amazed by the

133

Sally Gates

mongrel's kindness to the underdog. Just as he frequently acts as the ears and eyes of his owner, he will do the same for his canine friends. Sally Gates, a Woolly Whitejaw from Leamington Spa, disliked other bitches and used to grumble quietly when she passed them. She did however have a male Poodle friend called Peppi who always accompanied Sally and her mistress on their evening walk. Eventually Peppi went blind, but Sally, with typical mongrel tenacity, was determined they should still enjoy their romps in the meadow. She would stand quite still until Peppi placed his black head against her back leg, then off they would go as one dog.

Nor is this an isolated example. Prince Hale, a Fox Terrier/Greyhound cross would take Mrs Hale's aunt's dog for a walk, holding the lead in his mouth. While Candy Morton, a black Alsatian cross, befriended a blind and ancient Great Dane who often came to stay in her house in Daventry, taking her down the garden when she wanted to have a pee, and bringing her back later. Sally Lilley, a Borderline Collie, also shows typical sheepdog protectiveness towards her deaf Labrador friend Ricky. Once when the family was walking in the Lake District, Ricky got lost. Being deaf, he couldn't hear his frantic owners calling. Sally quietly disappeared, and emerged a few minutes later from the bullrushes. Much to everyone's relief, she was leading a dripping and bewildered Ricky.

Sally Lilley

Whenever we have owned male pedigree dogs, they have always developed a penchant for a male mongrel dog. Simon, one of the Golden Retrievers of my childhood, had a Standard Magpie admirer called Cresswell with whom he used to fornicate for hours outside my father's office. Later they fell out over a bitch and never spoke to one another again.

In the same way Maidstone, our Setter, when he was a gawky adolescent, formed a passionate attachment for another Standard Magpie called Capon who used to call on him most mornings, accompany us on our walks, and initiate Maidstone into the delights of fornication and hunting. Later when Maidstone grew to doghood, and started fancying bitches, Capon lost interest and took up with another adolescent breed dog.

My grandfather's hideously ugly mongrel Evans, on the other hand, had a male friendship which lasted until death. Every day the friend would pick Evans up in the morning. They would saunter down to the station and, presumably with the blessing of the stationmaster, catch the little train two stops down the valley to the beech woods, spend all day hunting, and catch the train back in the evening.

134

It is interesting too to watch dogs initiating each other into hunting rituals. Barbara and Fortnum rely entirely on Mabel's sense of smell to locate the best voles and field mice.

Mrs Crook of Tring already owned a Borderline Collie called Jess, and just before Christmas acquired a six-month-old Jack Russell called Kim. Jess took to Kim immediately, showing him all her haunts in the woods, and teaching him to hunt as she does by chasing flat out – an odd thing for a Jack Russell to learn. Kim, in return, has taught her his own style of hunting, which is digging obsessively at a likely hole. Jess, with her long legs, is a very cumbersome digger, and Kim gets very impatient and swears at her; so she stands back and lets him get on with it, just giving a cursory scratch from time to time to show she's still in the hunt.

Chip Smith, the original Black and Tan Tightskin from Kingston, found his new home by turning up on Mr Smith's doorstep nine years ago and refusing to leave. Chip has one dog friend, a huge black Satin Crammer who frequently turns up at the house and takes Chips off courting and dustbinning, sometimes for several days on the trot. Despite his obvious devotion, however, little Chip has all the social insecurity of the rescued dog and is obviously slightly ashamed of his rough friend. He never allows him into the house, or even up the alley-way leading up to the back door. Feeling guilty of such snobbish disloyalty, perhaps, Chip makes it up to his friend by ferociously picking fights with every other black male dog in the district. As Chip never attacks yellow, red or white dogs, this behaviour must be to underline the fact that he's not discriminating against his friend.

Most impressive, however, is the way mongrels sometimes save their dog friends' lives. Mrs Braddell of Bude in Cornwall owned a black Spaniel and a fox-eared Shagpile called Sambo. One day the Spaniel had a stroke. While she was lying motionless in her basket, Sambo turned up with a tennis ball which he proceeded to bounce from his mouth until she began to show signs of interest. After that she soon recovered and lived another eleven years.

Another story of courage came from Mrs Taylor who lived on the edge of a huge forest. Her goldy-red Satin Crammer, Pancho, used to dive into the wood and go hunting with his mate Crusoe. One afternoon, the forest keeper carried Pancho into the house saying the dog's paw had been caught in a trap. Despite the terrible pain, Pancho had luckily had the sense not

Sambo Braddell

135

to pull it out. Crusoe had barked frantically for help until the keeper, hearing the din, came and released him.

Mr Harold Knight of Capel le Ferrie, Folkestone, also describes an incident just after the Second World War when two mongrel cronies used to walk past his house every day. One night he and his wife were kept awake until dawn by dogs barking continuously. 'Next morning,' wrote Mr Knight, 'a neighbour and I went across the fields and found one of the dogs had entangled his shaggy tail in the barbed wire. My neighbour fetched a pair of wire cutters and we managed to free the wretched dog – a very dodgy business I remember; the fact that the second dog stayed by his pal all night, assisting in the barking, deserves a mention.'

Scamp Doubleday

Most heartrending of all is the way the mongrel mourns the death of a beloved dog friend. Scamp Doubleday, a pale chestnut Lancashire Hot Pet with huge eyes, a white shirt front and curling black ears, had a Poodle bitch friend called Mandy whom she collected each day for a walk. Alas, Mandy got run over, and her mistress Mrs Hamilton (intending to bury the dog when her husband came home that evening) left her under a blanket by the back door. Scamp, arriving as usual to collect her friend, went into a frenzy of distress, pulling the blanket off Mandy, howling all the time, and trying to lie on top of her and warm some life back into her. Even when Mrs Hamilton tried to hold down the blanket with bricks, little Scamp pushed them aside and went on crying like a baby.

After three or four hours of dragging her away, Mrs Hamilton decided to bury Mandy herself. She waited until Scamp crept miserably back home, then dug a deep hole in the back garden. When she had lowered Mandy into the grave and was starting to cover her with earth, back came Scamp and jumped into the grave, howling like Hamlet, and as fast as Mrs Hamilton buried Mandy, Scamp dug her up. In the end Mrs Hamilton gave in, and left the two dogs together until dark. When her husband came home, and Scamp was well and truly locked up, they buried Mandy. Scamp mourned her friend for weeks but Mrs Doubleday took her for extra walks, and gradually she seemed to get over it.

It will have been noticed that the lion's share of dogs in this chapter have been Satin Crammers, who probably have a high proportion of Labrador blood in their make-up. Intense friendliness and sweetness of temperament are, of course, typical Labrador characteristics, a classic example of which can be found in the poignant story of Andy Crook of Tring, yet another black

136

Satin Crammer, Andy was a compulsive philanderer until his mistress brought him home a little blond Fox Dog friend called Frisky. Although she was spayed, they became such friends that Andy didn't go bitching again for twelve years. Last year however Frisky died at the great age of seventeen. Although the Crooks took Andy everywhere with them, he was inconsolable. By this time he was sixteen, half blind and deaf. One Sunday morning in June he suddenly disappeared. Rewards were offered. The police, the dogs' home and every vet in the district were notified, but Andy never came home.

'Did he revert to bitching,' writes Mrs Crook, 'or did he go looking for Frisky?' Perhaps like Captain Oates he knew he was going to die, and with great chivalry took himself off on his own so as not to bother anyone. Sadly his mistress will never know.

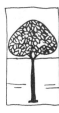

Chapter 16

Mongrels and other animals

My own three mongrels do not have a good track record with other animals. Perhaps they have too much Terrier or Greyhound blood in their make-up. Although they live in comparative harmony with our four cats at home, outside the house they will chase anything that moves: neighbours' cats, guinea pigs, rabbits, squirrels, ducks, hens, nothing is safe. When I go to the country I always arm myself with at least £15 in cash – not to tip the servants, but to pacify enraged local farmers for any livestock killed off. Many a time Fortnum has proudly returned with a huge ginger moustache, having successfully raided the nearest chicken coop. Individually, however, they are cowards and will only kill as a pack.

Such delinquency, I'm glad to say, is not common in mongrels, although many with Terrier blood will chase cats. Roberta Werson of Southall, for example, a shaggy Borderline Collie with a touch of Airedale, hated the heat and on warm summer nights preferred to sleep out in the garden tethered to a table. In the middle of one night her owners were woken by a harrowing din of screeching and barking. Roberta had dispatched a visiting tomcat with such vigour that she'd broken the table, dragging her own half with its two legs down the garden, and finally coming to a noisy halt when it wedged in the fence.

Other dogs can only take cats in small doses. Bruce Jackson, a black Satin Crammer from Broadstairs, tolerated the family cat, but was very put out when she produced kittens. To his relief all were found homes except one, who slept in a box in the kitchen. One evening Bruce's mistress found the box empty, and after searching the house, just in time she discovered the kitten fast asleep in the middle of a frosty lawn. Bruce couldn't bring himself to kill it, but, like the Eskimo putting his grandmother out on the ice-floe, felt it would have been all right to let it freeze to death.

Duffy Townsend

Rip Cowhig

Tib Brown

Mongrels also tend to be extremely nosy. A General Wolfe-hound called Duffy Townsend, from Wisbech, was obsessed by the new goldfish in the garden pond. After spending weeks frustrating Duffy's attempts to get them out, his mistress came back from the shops to find he had laid all the fish out on the lawn, and was patting them with his paw. When scolded he looked up reproachfully, as if to say he didn't want to eat her wretched fish, just find out what they felt like. He never touched them again.

The majority of mongrels, perhaps because so many of them these days have Collie or gundog blood, are incredibly kind and protective towards other animals. Rip Cowhig, for example, a beautiful Twentieth Century Fox Dog the colour of autumn leaves, loved all cats but was particularly fond of Buster, the cat who lived in the same house. One balmy summer evening, despite a badly cut and bandaged foot, Rip persuaded his mistress to go for a walk. Buster joined them as usual. Suddenly, from the shadows of a side street, jumped three Alsatians, cornering poor Buster against a wall with ferocious growls. Hearing the commotion the lionhearted Rip, fury fuelled by devotion, leapt to the rescue and, despite his wounded paw, saw all three Alsatians off with their tails between their legs. Whereupon Buster strolled up to his brave, panting friend and gave him a nonchalant congratulatory lick on the cheek.

Rip was devastated when Buster died, but eventually found a replacement in a tiny black kitten whom he discovered with her head jammed between the spokes of a bicycle wheel. Rip's mistress adopted the kitten and called her Gypsy. After Rip died, Gypsy in her turn was inconsolable, vanishing for five days in a desperate search for her old friend. What was touching was that when she returned, a neighbouring dog called Snowy (who normally detested cats and dispatched any dog that entered his road) sensed Gypsy's desolation and came up to the house every day to sit with her in silent sympathy until she got over her period of mourning.

The mongrel will frequently display far more maternal feeling for kittens than a mother cat. Tib Brown, a Borderline Collie from Blackpool, carried home a family of stray kittens she'd found in a derelict building and proceeded to bring them up, washing and suckling them, and if they strayed too far from her basket gently bringing them back in her mouth. Even more remarkably, male dogs will sometimes take on the maternal role. Simon Ledger, for example, a black Satin Crammer, took total control of a litter of kittens when their flighty mother aban-

140

doned them on frequent returns to the tiles. While Fred Grimes, a Rough-and-Reddish, always fetched in the family kittens at night, rounding them up and gently nudging them up the path.

One of the saddest aspects of owning a dog is that you cannot explain death, or how long you're going to be away, to them. Poor Sambo Braddell, an adorable fox-eared Shagpile seen in chapter 15 bouncing a ball to rouse his Spaniel stable mate out of a stroke, was also very fond of a ginger cat called Trigger. After Trigger died, Sambo refused to eat for a week, and went out in search of him, coming back with his face covered in scratches, presumably from asking other cats if they knew where Trigger had gone.

Mongrels' intelligence should never be underestimated. Shadow Robertson, a beautiful blond Shagpile, loved the family kitten and was inconsolable when it had to be put down. She looked everywhere for it, and for three days after Mrs Robertson threw out the kitten's basket, glared at her reproachfully.

'When I could stand it no longer,' writes Mrs Robertson, 'I sat all four-and-a-half-stone of Shadow on my lap, and explained what had happened. Somehow she seemed to understand that I was as upset as she was, and instantly forgave me and licked my face again.'

Mongrels will also assume responsibility for anyone who belongs to a family, saying, like Ruth, 'Your creatures shall be my creatures.' Russ Vear, a brindle Prop Forward, used to go round his estate every morning inspecting the livestock like a lord of the manor. They included two rabbits, two tortoises, three golden pheasants, two budgerigars, two cockatoos, and twenty-one ex-battery hens revelling in a new found freedom, not to mention two kittens who loved him dearly. Russ even made the same tour the day he died, at the great age of sixteen.

Skippy Whapham, a youthful Wooly Whitejaw, loves lambs and always mothers the orphans that are bottlefed in the house, keeping all the other dogs away. Tina Wood, an enchanting Half Cocker from Towcester, discovered a dying lamb in the hedgerow and barked until her mistress carried it home, whereupon Tina took over, licking the lamb back to life and snuggling up to it in her basket. Tina also made friends with the resident hens, and dug in their run, kindly unearthing worms for them (and the odd bone for herself). One particular hen and she became the best of friends, and often had a tug of war over a bone. Without any prompting from her owners, Tina even taught herself to collect the new-laid eggs and carry them into the house. She never broke one.

Tina Wood

141

Rags Ford, a little Rough and Reddish from Hampton Hill, had a passion for day-old chicks, and used to stretch out on the lawn, letting them cuddle up to him and explore his thick hairy coat. Brackie Leete, a huge wonderfully worried-looking brindle Boxer cross from Germany, befriended a baby duckling and didn't even grumble one day when the duckling mistook her rather long teats for worms.

Time and again, too, one is amazed by the commonsense and sheer unselfishness of the mongrel. Prince Sampson of Sidcup, a handsome black Satin Crammer, lived with a family of tame rabbits. One day when they were all out in their runs, there was a cloudburst. In an exploit worthy of Beatrix Potter, Prince removed all the rabbits from the run – including a doe and her babies – and rounded them up underneath their hutches. When his owners got home poor Prince was absolutely drenched, but the rabbits were warm and dry. Shaun Skillen of Guisely, a handsome Pied Wagtail, used to guard thirteen guinea pigs, washing them, playing with them and fiercely fighting off any neighbouring dog who popped in for a quick snack.

Mongrels are also bright enough to draw the line between home and away creatures. Flash Brooks, a jaunty white Prop Forward, always chased rabbits when out on walks, but was devoted to the tame rabbits kept by his family. If they ever escaped from their hutches when the family was out, he would round them up, yapping anxiously until a neighbour came to investigate and put them back.

Mongrels also have a sense of fair play. George Bieliki, a little red Lancashire Hot Pet living in Porchester Square, was a compulsive rabbit chaser, but would never touch a doe if she was with her babies. Josh Lewis of Basingstoke, a beautiful ginger Borderline Collie, rushed into a thicket one day to investigate a rustling of leaves. Suddenly there was a shriek of pain, and Josh rushed out limping pathetically, having been seen off by a baby rabbit.

Some dogs even feel they should guard birds which are quite capable of making their own escape. Trixie Hubbard spent much of her life refereeing a Tweetie Pie-Pussy Cat power-struggle between the resident cat and budgerigar. One day the budgie escaped and flew into the garden, where the cat was waiting licking its lips on top of a rabbit hutch. As it started stalking the budgie, Trixie flew at the cat knocking it out of the way. The budgie lives on. Alas, Trixie had to be put down when she was seventeen-and-a-half.

142

Patch Kielty of Leeds, a splendidly piratical Borderline Collie with a huge plumed tail, was a rescued dog himself. As a puppy, he was found floating down the river with his legs tied together, clinging desperately to a piece of wood. He obviously feels that other living things deserve a second chance too. Known in the local press as 'Patch the Saviour', he was walking through the churchyard one day when he scattered a group of starlings who appeared to be pecking something to death. It turned out to be a budgerigar soaked with rain and on its last claws. Patch carried it gently to his master who took it home and revived it. Later Patch rescued an injured linnet and a wood pigeon. He also acts as a lollipop dog to all the local children, barking when they try to cross the road when there's a car coming. Another Patch, this time a grey Rough Diamond from Penrith called Patch Wilson, loved to watch the moorhens swimming with their chicks when she went on walks round a nearby lake. On several occasions she dived into the water and chased off stoats that were trying to eat the chicks, and got a bloody nose for her pains.

Trixie Thomson

My favourite story about mongrels and birds however was sent in by Mrs Thomson of Watford. Her blond Edith Sitwell, Trixie, always liked something to mother. First it was Mrs Thomson's children whom she escorted back and forth to school, then it was her own puppies. When the Thomsons moved to the country Trixie started vanishing every morning, and did not return until tea time. As she was always there at weekends, they decided she must have found herself a nine to five job. One day Mrs Thomson's son squeezed through the fence after Trixie, and followed her to a small bungalow some doors away where she barked at the door and was let in. He rushed home to tell Mrs Thomson, who went round to see what Trixie was up to. The owner ushered her in. There was Trixie stretched out in front of a blazing fire with a budgerigar perched on her head. She totally ignored Mrs Thomson and went back to sleep again. It appeared that the bungalow owner's spaniel had died a few months before; next day Trixie had moved in.

Chapter 17

Working mongrels

Apart from his sterling work guarding a family and keeping the household running smoothly, the versatile mongrel often takes a second job to stop himself turning into a cabbage – not a vegetable of which he's particularly fond. We have just seen how Trixie Thomson left home every day from nine to five to budgerigar-sit in a nearby bungalow. Back in the thirties, Nigger Taylor, a delectable General Wolfehound acquired for five shillings from Battersea Dogs' Home, found employment several days a week working as a sweeper's mate. Each morning he would wait patiently by the front door for the local road sweeper to collect him and take him on his rounds. Nigger would then walk solemnly beside the handcart, sit down between stops, and always be returned home safely at the end of the morning. Much of his afternoon would then be spent resting from his labours in his hammock in the garden.

Nigger Taylor

Spot Whincup, a contemporary mongrel, didn't even have to be collected for work, but turned up regularly to accompany one particular North Chingford road sweeper on his rounds. On the day the road sweeper retired, Spot retired too in sympathy, but within a few months, obviously bored by inactivity, he was out on the streets again, bemusing the new road sweeper with his attentions. Alas the job didn't work out. A week or so later Spot was seen accompanying the local postman round the neighbourhood.

Pancho Taylor, the Satin Crammer who in an earlier chapter was seen catching his paw in a trap in the woods, was soon back doing a full day's work in the country. Every morning Eddie the postman would collect him from home, and he would follow Eddie's bicycle for the first round of the day, then go back to the sorting depot for lunch. After lunch, Pancho would do a round in the GPO van, diligently guarding the mail. One day, however, he literally deserted his post by leaping out of the stationary van after a pigeon. Poor Eddie looked for him every-where, but in the end had to return to the Taylors empty-handed, saying he'd lost their dog. Fortunately Pancho had a good sense of direction, and returned the ten miles home before dusk. It seems fitting – since they were so devoted to one another – that Eddie and Pancho died at the same time.

Bitches, unlike dogs, tend not to wander from home, but Snappy Tober, a Black and Tan Tightskin, still manages to help the postman in her quiet way. When he walks up the path, she lifts the flap of the letter-box with her paw so that he can slide the letters through. While Emma Ball (a merry Twentieth Century Fox Dog from Brenchley in Kent) helps out her family in their village shop, which is also a sub-post office. From 6 a.m. onwards, when her master is manning the store on his own, Emma acts as his early warning system. If he's in the kitchen when a customer comes in, she gives not her usual rousing bark which might scare people off, but just a quiet woof of 'shop' to let him know someone needs serving.

Other mongrels, unwilling ever to be parted from their owners, insist on accompanying them to work. Many Esdaile, a Bertrand Russell, belonged to a schoolmaster, attended every lesson and was an excellent example to the pupils as he curled up motionless in the corner of the classroom. Meg Stoker, a beautiful Vertical Shagpile, always came to school where her mistress was teaching art, often had her portrait painted, and particularly enjoyed accompanying the children on sketching club outings.

Offices are also often enhanced by the presence of a mongrel. Seamus, a Northern Ireland Shagpile, goes to work regularly and helps the typists to slim by eating their biscuits. Rusty Harris, an Old Sea Dog and mighty warrior, and his side-kick Basil, a Twentieth Century Fox Dog, not only guard their mistress's property company, but also accompany her on her rounds collecting rent. Even the most shady tenants never give her any trouble. One look at Rusty's saturnine countenance and they pay up.

Barney Leete-Hodge, the Jack Russell who leaves the room when his mistress undresses, also disapproves of her job as a publisher's editor. He likes it on the days when she settles down in her office at home, because it means she won't be going out without him, but insists on sitting on top of her filing cabinet in order to keep an eye on the street outside. He then waits until she's just answering the telephone, then barks at a cat at which he's been gazing for half an hour. He hates her typing even

146

more, peering at her furiously for the first few minutes, then stumping off to unmake her bed.

Nor does Mrs Loverock of Findern, Derbyshire, find her cat-hating mongrel, Spot the greatest business asset. When she tours the neighbourhood selling Avon make-up, Spot, a very sharp Jack Russell, waits till she's gone out then nips smartly through the cat door, and, excellent ratter that she is, tunnels a hole under the fence big enough for herself. She then scales the neighbour's high fence and charges after Mrs Loverock, joining her on the doorstep of her first client with the joyous shout of Avon barking.

Spot Loverock

In his book *My Dog Tulip*, J. R. Ackerley wrote of Tulip's mongrel boyfriend, Watney, who lived in the pub and whose job it was to guard the till and ring the bell at closing time, duties which he totally neglected when Tulip was on heat. Whiskey Evans, a Borderline Collie of great character, took his duties as pub dog much more seriously. At opening time, he would hang over the first-floor balcony monitoring every customer entering or leaving the pub, then creep downstairs under the bar, and on the call of 'Last orders please' put his feet on the bar and keep barking until everyone left.

Bouncer de Lory, the Romney Marshall sketched by Konrad Lorenz, had a mistress whose mother practised as a psychiatrist. Bouncer wanted to be a psychiatrist too, but believed in shock treatment. He used to hide under the couch, and give the patients very real traumas by scrambling out unexpectedly during sessions and bouncing all over them. Heavy industry, as well, is often livened up by the mongrel. Scamp Neighbour of Henley-on-Thames (*see* p. 144), a Borderline Collie, often wins prizes for the Happiest Dog. During the week his master, who is a carpenter, takes Scamp to work on a building site, signing in as 'one carpenter and one dog.' Scamp's job includes digging up the newly-laid lawns, walking across wet concrete, leaving his paw prints behind, and guarding the finished houses so that prospective buyers cannot look over them. He also loves riding in the digger, and hitching a lift in the wheel-barrow if the digger isn't in use. Scamp's pay for a week's work is a bag of bones from the local butcher. After his day he's so tired that he has his dinner, and then sleeps all night. If it rains he gets left behind and mopes all day.

One of the most touching dog rescue stories came to me anonymously from a man who works for a firm of house-clearing contractors in Cheshire. One day, after some long-term squatters had been thrown out of a derelict house, this man and

147

his work mates were ordered to move in and 'butcher' the place. They were just boarding up the windows when they heard a faint whimper. It took nearly an hour to find an old-fashioned hat box on top of a wardrobe. Inside shivered a half-starved puppy about seven weeks old. Happily, from that moment the puppy's luck changed. Re-named Hatter, he became a pet of the contractors and was kept in the yard, given a hut of his own, but never tied up. Although Hatter guards his yard fiercely, he's also a great favourite with the local children who all take him for walks.

Back in the twenties, another little mongrel called Monty Trott ambitiously established himself as resident guard dog at the Tower of London. Given as a puppy to the newly appointed curator of the crown jewels, Monty was soon very popular with both staff and tourists. Even the Royal Family asked after him when they visited the Tower. On one memorable occasion, the alarm system had just been renewed in the Wakefield Tower. At the opening ceremony, the great doors were opened and the alarm switched on. An official was about to cross the threshold with great solemnity to test the rays, when suddenly little Monty, determined to steal the limelight, trotted ahead of him. To everyone's consternation no alarm sounded as the little dog passed through. It was only triggered off by the official. To general hilarity it was then discovered that the rays didn't reach the floor. To stop thieves crawling through on their stomachs, they were subsequently readjusted.

In the country, of course, the working mongrel really does get the chance to prove his worth. Teddy Williams, an enchanting pre-war Rough Diamond, used to trot down to his master's chicken farm every day, climb the ladder to the nesting boxes, collect the eggs in a basket, and carry them a mile back to the house. He never broke one.

A train ran through his master's land, and the guard used to chuck the morning paper into the fields for Teddy to collect. Tragically, one day the guard forgot to throw it out. Perplexed, Teddy hared after the train, drew ahead, and in a heroic attempt to remind the guard, crossed in front of the train, losing a back leg and receiving a deep gash in the head. One of the local vets was called in to put him out of his misery, but when Teddy gazed up at him with pleading eyes, he said, 'I simply can't do it. The dog's in terrible pain, but he's begging me to save him.'

The vet was right. Teddy recovered with incredible speed, resumed his duties on three legs with as much gusto as ever and lived to be nineteen.

148

Joe Lee, the slim grey Twentieth Century Fox Dog with strange yellow eyes who was seen in chapter 6 enjoying a clandestine tryst in the loft with his master's Collie bitch, was very unhappy when he first arrived to live with the Lees. Nervous and aggressive, he kept rushing back to his first owners who were about to emigrate to Australia. The moment his new master put him to work on the farm, however, he settled down and was perfectly happy. He knew instinctively what to do, and was frightened of nothing. He could face a great bullock and turn it, or be gentleness itself with young lambs, holding each one down with his paw to help Mr Lee catch and dose it. He also brought in the cows for milking and would accompany the sheep along the road, dashing ahead to wait in gate-ways, standing on his hind legs to see what was happening up front, and even going over the sheep's backs like an Australian kelpie.

Joe Lee

After dark one evening a neighbour rang up to say one of Mr Lee's lambs was bleating its head off in a field behind the village. When Joe and his master reached the spot and found the lamb, it had somehow landed up on the other side of the river, and stood crying in the circle of torchlight. Instantly Joe dived into the river, swam across, coaxed the lamb into the water, and swam back with it, all the time in pitch dark except for the light of the torch.

On another occasion four sheep had got themselves on the wrong side of the river in daylight. Mr Lee sent Sue, the official farm sheepdog, over to collect them, but having swum across she got cold feet, and sat on the far bank whimpering and refusing to move. Once again mongrel Joe rushed to the rescue, swimming across, helping Sue coax the sheep back into the river, and shoving them off the bank with his front paws, so that finally sheep and dogs all swam back together.

Later Mr and Mrs Lee moved to the Quantocks and started a riding and holiday centre. Once again Joe was in his element, running up and down between house and stables, bringing in the horses from the fields, making the visitors feel at home, rounding up the bantams for penning in the evening, helping to train the young dogs, and letting his master and mistress know if anything was wrong.

Daisy Coutts

'We had children staying and riding from all over the world, and coming back year after year,' writes Mrs Lee. 'Everyone of them remembers Smoky Joe with great affection.'

Another highly skilled farmpaw is little Daisy Coutts, a white Bertrand Russell with a chestnut patch over one eye, who lives in the New Forest. One of the Forest rules is that cattle, ponies

149

Blackleg

and pigs have the right to pasture at random. Daisy's master and mistress milk a dairy herd, and if any cows from a different herd stray up to the gate, Daisy recognizes them instantly and sends them packing. The Coutts also own four sows. Whenever they are fed over the front gate, Daisy supervises their dinner as strictly as any Norland Nanny. If a strange sow tries to muscle in before they've finished up, Daisy will see it off noisily. Down by the river, her master has some filbert nut bushes. Left alone, squirrels would clear the lot every year, but without any prompting Daisy goes on squirrel patrol in the autumn and spends hours under the bushes driving off invaders. As soon as the nuts are picked, she ignores the bushes completely.

Judging by Daisy's performance, bitches can hold down a demanding job as easily as dogs. Another triumph for Bitches' Lib was Susie of Battersea. Anyone who visited the Home until a few years ago would have been surprised to see a little black and white Family Circler called Susie charging about as though she owned the place. Susie's story is a sad one which ended happily. For many years she was the devoted companion of an

150

old lady who finally, at the age of eighty-two, set fire to her bed by accident in the middle of the night. Susie promptly raised the alarm by barking her head off, and saved the old lady's life by tugging the burning sheets and blankets off her bed.

The old lady recovered in hospital, and agreed to go to an old people's home, but was terribly distressed about abandoning Susie. She was only comforted when Battersea informed her that the bitch would end her days in the Home as official guard dog. Susie soon attached herself to one of the keepers and made herself very useful by rounding up any dog that got loose, and barking until a member of the staff returned it to its pen. She reached a good age before she died one night in her sleep.

Battersea also tells a poignant story of how one of the great mongrel workers was re-united with its owner. Up to the counter one day came a hard-faced harpy, inches deep in make-up, and wearing an extremely revealing dress. She was looking for a little brown and white Terrier, she said. Full of curiosity, one of the keepers followed her on a search down the dog lines.

Suddenly a small Bertrand Russell went wild in its pen, and started to bark and scrabble frantically at the bars. Next moment the harpy, abandoning her pose of indifference, rushed to the dog, crying tears of pure joy until her rouge and her purple mascara were streaked down her cheeks, and her false eyelashes had both fallen off.

'Forgive my curiosity,' said the keeper, as he handed over the ecstatic dog, 'but you don't strike me as the sort of person who'd break down over an old mongrel.'

'Well,' said the lady, shrugging, 'the little bugger's my bread and bu'er, ain't he? I'm on the game, you see. If I have 'im on a lead with me at night, the cops never pick me up.'

Chapter 18

Holidays

Mongrels, being adaptable, are excellent companions on holiday. Any dog owner who has endured the frightful swallowing and reproachful glances when suitcases are packed will also be familiar with the frantic ecstasy when the lead is placed on top of the suitcases or inside the car and the dog realizes that he's included in the excursion. Peter Warlow, a little black Borderline Collie from Portsmouth, always assumed he was coming too, and collected his brush and towels to be packed with his owner's things. And if anyone mentions the word 'holiday' to Lassie of Sutton, she rushes off and brings her little suitcase to be packed.

A white and gold Fetcher called Lady Burroughs, on the other hand, took a day or two to adjust when her family took her caravanning for the first time. They hadn't packed her basket, so she spent most of the first night reproachfully commuting between Mr and Mrs Burroughs and their daughter, waking them up with a small wet nose pushed into their faces to 'see if they were all right.' Finally they were roused in the early hours by terrible barking and yelping. Imagining robbers, they rushed into the kitchen next door to find Lady growling ferociously at a huge grasshopper, which she thought was going to hurt them. When the grasshopper was evicted, the Burroughs finally got to bed with 'one faithful companion convinced she was the heroine of the hour, having routed the intruder.'

Some mongrels enjoy an energetic holiday. Bret Gordon, a fine Borderline Collie, for example, went backpacking in the Highlands with his master and had his own back pack in which he carried his food and his bed. Most dogs however prefer a seaside vacation. It is seldom too hot for dogs in England, and the beach offers plenty of picnics to shake sand over, and also endless scavenging possibilities. Toby Spice, an Old Sea Dog and an incorrigible escaper, invariably deserted his owners on

Lady Burroughs

153

Mandy Halliday

the beach and homed in on old ladies, standing trembling and forlorn at their feet until, imagining him lost, they gave him most of their sandwiches. Other dogs enjoy bathing in the sea and keeping a watch over their owners at the same time. Bob Giles, a Borderline Collie with a white tipped tail which never stopped wagging, realized his mistress was frightened of water and swam round and round her, giving her confidence all the time she was in the water. He also guarded clothes and 'could knock a large beach ball back into your hands with his head, keeping it up for ages'. Mandy Halliday, a platinum blond smooth Twentieth Century Fox Dog, was also a beach ball fanatic, particularly excelling in goal. After every holiday she had a bare nose from dribbling.

Mrs Somerville, who is now eighty-five, remembers a summer holiday seventy-five years ago when her family were bathing in a very rough sea. Don, their Ebony Fetcher, although a powerful swimmer decided it was too choppy and stayed on the beach.

'Suddenly my mother vanished,' writes Mrs Somerville. 'Without a moment's hesitation, Don dived into the water and seized her hand, and wouldn't let go until she was safely on land. Actually she had said to my brothers, "How deep are we? I will go down until my feet touch sand, and then hold up my hand; when you see it disappear dive after me," but of course Don got there first.'

Buster Davies, an enchanting black and tan Romney Marshall, on the other hand, detested the water and was outraged when his mistress, in an attempt to teach him to swim, threw him into the sea. Bolting up the beach, he avoided her for half an hour, and was only coaxed back to good temper by the biggest ice cream available from the Tonibell van.

Bobby Booth, the Bertrand Russell whom we have already met as 'the President of the Buggers' Club' in chapter 6, was also an embarrassment to his mistress on holiday. Once while at the seaside they passed a very beautiful girl who was sunbathing face downwards. She was attended by a much coiffed Maltese Terrier with a large blue bow on his forelock who was gazing out to sea. Bobby took one look at this shining example of pedigree imbecility, then trotted up and pee-ed all over the Maltese Terrier's head. The blue ribbon became wetter and wetter and finally drooped over his face. The silly dog didn't even seem to notice.

On every beach you will find a local beachcomber – or animated litter bin. Scamp, a little rough mongrel, belongs to the

154

whole village of Gortonhaven and enhances everyone's holiday. The theory locally is that he was left behind one year when his visiting owners couldn't be bothered to take him home. Now he sleeps at the local pub, but first thing every morning he hares down to the beach and stays there all day, attaching himself to various friendly groups and avoiding Bert, the beach attendant, who thinks he should be tied up.

Dogs, like people, also have holiday romances, but in the mongrel's case these romances are sometimes more durable.

Mrs Glover of Lincolnshire wrote of a very touching friendship which grew up between Tosca, her Family Circler, and Prince, the local beachcomber. Prince had learned to live by his wits. In summer he haunted the beaches, charming tourists into sharing their picnics, and into throwing pebbles for him to chase. In winter he was a town dog, with an extensive knowledge of the back entrances of all the cafés with sympathetic owners in the district. He only acknowledged his home when food was scarce, or when it was very cold. The police knew him and left him alone. Every time he met Tosca he greeted her with ecstasy, and accompanied her on every walk for five years, until the day she died.

Holidays, however, are not always happy times for dogs. Criminally irresponsible owners, who can't be bothered to pay someone to look after them, often turf them out on the streets, or let them loose in the country or, wickedest of all, dump them on a motorway. Another ploy is to take off your dog's identity disc and get a friend to take him to the local dogs' home as a stray. When you return from holiday, you go to the home and pick out your dog with every demonstration of simulated amazement at finding him, having received seven days' free board and lodging.

Other more responsible owners send their dogs to kennels. But this seems to have a more detrimental effect on mongrels than on breed dogs. The rescued dog, in particular, can become absolutely demented. As was pointed out in an earlier chapter, he tends to resent any confinement to barracks, and if shoved into a strange prison surrounded by barking dogs, he automatically assumes he's been sent back once more to the concentration camp of the dogs' home. In *Jimmy, The Dog In My Life*, Sir Arthur Bryant tells of the time he left Jimmy, a rescued beachcomber, in a London Dog Parlour for a couple of hours to be clipped. When Sir Arthur picked him up, Jimmy was so shellshocked with distress that he was unable for a while to get his bearings or realize where he was.

155

Pip Martin-Royle

Dusty Ireland

To my eternal regret, I put Fortnum, with Maidstone, the Setter, into kennels when he was about a year old. My husband and I had to go to Africa for ten days, and in the meantime our kitchen was being completely gutted and rebuilt. It seemed unfair to expect a young and newish nanny to cope with five cats, two young children, two moderately uncontrollable dogs and an eviscerated kitchen all on her own. Ten days later, when we collected the dogs from the kennels, Maidstone was comparatively unaffected but Fortnum was skin and bones. He hadn't eaten since he'd been admitted, and had howled without stopping. It took me days to win back his confidence, and it was on his return from that visit that he seriously took up fighting.

One Bertrand Russell, Pip Martin-Royle, barked so continually during her fortnight's incarceration that when her owners picked her up she could only croak with excitement because she'd completely lost her voice.

The great mongrel escape artists will always refuse to be contained. Pip (male this time) Higgins, a handsome red Fetcher with a touch of Alsatian, came originally from Liverpool Dogs' Home, and was determined never to be imprisoned again. On all five occasions he was put in kennels he managed to escape, clearing a six-foot mesh wire fence in the process. The kennel maids nicknamed him 'Houdini', and always claimed they were going to get out the cross and nails next time he was booked in.

Paddy England, a smoky grey Romney Marshall, also came from a dogs' home. He detested cats, and in pursuit of them turned the neighbours' back gardens into his own Grand National course, leaping high fence after high fence all along the street. He was obviously practising for a more serious occasion. Warned of his jumping prowess, the kennels felt, quite erroneously, that they could keep him in. The first night, he scaled a seven-foot fence and went straight home.

Chum Ferris, a Dalmatian/Wirehaired Terrier cross, went into kennels for two weeks while his owners went away. They decided to stay for an extra day's holiday, and when they got home they found Chum waiting on the doorstep. A few minutes later, one of the kennel maids rolled up looking very worried. Evidently Chum had behaved impeccably through his visit and had never made any attempt to get out until the last day. He must have heard Mrs Ferris say what day she was going to collect him.

Bearing in mind the fuss that mongrels make in kennels, it is not surprising that kennel owners don't like them very much. Miss Hefferman of Chigwell, who was three years a kennel maid, wrote that although half her charges were mongrels and the other half breed dogs, she was only bitten by mongrels.

'They were the most misbehaved and hardest to please,' she went on. 'For some reason, the owners of mongrel dogs see no need to train them; I'm sure some discipline would improve their image.' Perhaps once again the reason for this is that mongrels are so devoted to their owners that they tend to obey them out of desire to please, without needing any training. Deprived of the object of their love, they become bad tempered and insubordinate.

Mongrels also tend not to like kennels because they're often looked down on in favour of breed dogs. When Mrs Ireland went on holiday to Guernsey she tried to put Dusty, her extremely handsome ginger Family Circler, into kennels, but they made such a fuss about his not being a breed dog that she decided to take him with her instead, flying him out to Guernsey in a Viscount, which worked out cheaper anyway.

Whatever the reason, the mongrel bitterly resents being separated from his owners, particularly when they're off having a nice time. Paddy Wood, a little sherry coloured Shagpile with a wistful fox's face, looked far too pretty to be capable of recrimination, but nevertheless always punished her owners when they came home from holiday. Even though she'd been well fed, walked and cared for by Mrs Wood's son and daughter-in-law, she always sulked for at least a fortnight when her master and mistress came home, lurking in corners, and refusing to sit in the same room with them.

Mrs Marshall of Tisbury probably had the best solution to the problem:

'Our treasure Rover gave us seventeen years of happiness; in all those years we didn't take a holiday, as we couldn't bear to be parted from him.'

Paddy Wood

Rover Marshall

Chapter 19

Of shows and snobbery

Anyone who owns a mongrel must have experienced a sense of outrage at some time that his dog is banned from the Kennel Club. It is the same protective anger that any wife would feel if her hardworking, self-made husband were blackballed by some smart London Club for not having the right accent. The Kennel Club, not unlike the ancient aristocracy who regard any family founded after the Tudors as frightfully unsmart, is so determined to preserve its curless rapture that it refuses to recognize any breed that has existed for less than a hundred years. Consequently it won't accept Jack Russells or Lurchers, and has only just recognized the Border Collie as a legitimate breed. Rumour has it however that recently one of the Queen's Corgies mounted a Dachshund belonging to Princess Margaret without the benefit of the Royal Assent, and produced a litter of 'dorgies' which are so enchanting that Her Majesty has threatened to withdraw her patronage of the Kennel Club unless the breed receives recognition.

Unlike the breed dog, the poor mongrel has no exclusive shows from which all breed dogs are disqualified. Nor has he an exclusive Mongrel Club from which all breed dogs are banned, with its own set of rules:

1   All members must show at least eight different breeds in their pedigrees.

2   All members must have ransacked fifty dustbins.

3   All male members must have rogered at least seventeen breed bitches and all female members must have tripped up at least six breed dog owners in the previous year.

But whilst mongrel owners may feel sad that their dogs are banned from Crufts and all pedigree shows sanctioned by the Kennel Club, they should thank their lucky stars that mongrels have not been subjected to the same ghastly experimentation as breed dogs. Study the pedigree of any Crufts champion, and ten to one you will find a labyrinth of incestuous matings. To produce a successful show dog a highly esteemed breeding manual entitled *The Genetics of the Dog* even recommends mating brother to sister in every generation. It also provides a recommended sample pedigree in which the unfortunate puppy has two grandparents called Tim and Judy, who are also his great-grandparents on his mother's side. The ubiquitous Tim also turns up as another great-grandparent on the distaff side, and yet again as a great-great-grandparent. Not only would this be very much frowned on in the Prayer Book, but it is also liable to produce a race of matchless looking village idiots.

One is not denying that there are thousands of sensibly bred, intelligent pedigree dogs, but when you get avaricious, highly competitive breeders mating dogs with all the ruthlessness of vivisectionists merely to perfect one particular feature – the length of the nose, or the narrowness of the head – you will get dogs who are both zombies and physical cripples as well.

In *It's a Dog's Life*, Tim Heald wrote of a Boxer who is so nervous at shows that it won't eat, and has to be kept alive on three injections a day. One also sees breed dogs with displaced hips, hopelessly bandy legs buckling under huge bodies, eyes that are too big for the sockets, and squashed noses that impede their breathing horribly. Selective breeding for shorter tails in Beagles has produced dogs with fewer vertebrae and, eventually, spina bifida.

What one finds infuriating, too, is that despite the Kennel Club's contempt for mongrels and cross breeds, it will happily make use of them when necessary. Whenever an enterprising breeder wants to introduce a new coat colour, he simply crosses his precious pedigree dogs with any other dog of that special colour, irrespective of breed, and keeps on crossing until he gets the mixture right – a process that has been used during the formative period of almost every breed.

With pedigree puppies not even intended for the show ring costing £200 these days, it is hardly surprising that most Kennel Club sponsored shows are minefields of bitchiness and intrigue, full of butch lady breeders in tweed suits brandishing blow dryers. The comparatively few shows that do admit mongrels as well as breed dogs, however, are still great fun. They are slightly chaotic, like the pony club gymkhanas of the forties and fifties, with little girls being towed out of the ring by large dogs on the end of a piece of string. There are classes for the best kept

160

dog, the dog with the waggiest tail, the dog most like its owner, and the dog the judge would most like to take home, which, because even judges love an underdog, is usually won by a lovable mongrel. An open show that I visited in Richmond Park on Boxing Day recently, on the other hand, was held more on Kennel Club lines with the classes divided into Working, Non-Working and Most Appealing Dog. This show was particularly nice because, rather like the Caucus race, every dog entered was automatically presented with a red, white and blue rosette, so no one went home empty-handed. They needed some compensation. It was a brilliantly sunny but bitterly cold day, and the show was held for some reason in a little wood. Judging began about eleven thirty, but most of the owners who'd been there since ten o'clock had, despite drinking sherry out of a barrel, turned blue with cold. No one appeared to have any idea what was going on, and the three classes all got mixed up with one another as the dogs circled aimlessly, lifting their legs on the trees as they passed.

Among a fine turnout of Labradors, Setters, endless Springer Spaniels, Ridgebacks, and a beady looking Shih Tzuh with its hair tied up in a dinky bow, mongrels were very much in a minority. A couple of puppies with amber eyes and pale pink noses called Cassie and Rosie, whose father, according to the owner, was a Staffordshire Bull Terrier, and whose mother 'had put herself about', won fourth prize in the most appealing dog class. There was a little unpatrician-looking short-legged, long-tailed dog, who despite being led around by a very patrician-looking man in green gum boots was unplaced in the working dog class. The only other mongrel was a vast black Shagpile with long stalactites of silky hair hanging from his face and body, and breath rising in great white puffs from his shiny black nose. He was the one moving object who didn't look frozen as he gambolled round the wood, cannoning into working and non-working dogs like some rogue performer in an eightsome reel. No one in the crowd was in any doubt that this was the most appealing dog, and fortunately Terence Brady, the judge, agreed with them.

The dog called Sam Wright, who came from Hounslow, was so affectionate, extrovert and exuberant that he even upstaged his kennel mate, a lovely Red Setter, usually the most showy of breeds. His owner claimed that Sam was a mixture of Afghan, Dobermann and a Pyrenean Mountain Dog. He looked more like a gigantic Briard.

While writing this book, as I have already mentioned, I dis-

161

Sam Wright on his lap of honour

covered how certain physical types of mongrel display certain characteristics. The sharp little Terrier types tend to be aggressive and highly intelligent; the muscular tightskinned, stocky dogs clean up in the sex stakes; dogs with Collie blood excel in wisdom, intuition and looking after children and other animals. In the show ring, however, it is the Vertical Shagpiles like Sam Wright who, with their beauty and lovely phlegmatic natures, bring home the prizes.

Their great success is perhaps due to the current popularity of long-haired dogs which, in its turn, has no doubt been aided by the immense popularity of the Old English Sheepdog who appears on television.

Apparently in 1971 a Dulux rep at Crufts, hovering near two women watching an Old English Sheepdog class, overheard one say to the other, 'What breed are those beautiful dogs?'

'Oh, they're Duluxes,' replied the other knowledgeably, 'the paint dogs.'

162

The popularity of long hair must also have been helped by Dougal of *Magic Roundabout* fame, by a film frequently shown at Christmas about an Old English Sheepdog, called *Digby the Biggest Dog in the World*, and by Frank Muir's captivating Afghan 'What a Mess', the hero of his series of children's books. Significantly, too, the most popular breed in recent years has been the long-haired Yorkshire Terrier. Perhaps a final contributory factor is that we are moving into a new Victorian age, in which a dog is more acceptable if its sex is concealed behind long curtains of hair, like the floor-length table cloths covering Victorian table legs.

Nearly every letter I received proudly reporting success in the show ring included a photograph of a Vertical Shagpile. Pride of place, however, must go to Pippa Daniells (*see* p. 158), a black and white Shagpile, found as a puppy starving underneath a parked car, who has now won over seventy rosettes.

'She certainly catches the judges' eye,' said her mistress. 'I'm sure it's the way she looks at them.'

Another black and white Shagpile, William Bartlett of Tunbridge Wells, also knows how to gaze winningly at the judges. Among many other triumphs, he was the dog Michael Aspel most wanted to take home.

'It is charming to totter into vogue,' wrote Horace Walpole in the eighteenth century. He was referring to the fact that he'd just become the rage of smart French society at the advanced age of forty-eight. In the same way, Scamp Taylor of Loudwater took up showing when he was eleven-and-a-half. (This makes him over eighty in conventional 'dog years', which are calculated on the breed dog's life expectancy of ten calendar years.) He was entered in an agricultural dog show and won every class. Now, three and a half years later, he is the proud winner of over sixty rosettes, most of them firsts. A medium-sized iron grey Shagpile who was found starving in a dirty shed at five weeks old, Scamp always looks forward to his public appearances. After a bath and groom he waits by the car until his mistress is ready. Usually when he is in a car he barks at other dogs, but on show days he sits with his nose in the air and ignores all canines.

Other large dark grey Shagpiles include Sally Braby, who won a plaque and a rosette for being judged 'best overall dog' against strong pedigree competition at a show in Norfolk; Sam Carritt who wins 'happiest dog' prizes all over London; and Luke Maples, known as the 'doormat' who cleans up at all the Kent shows in the 'happiest dog' competitions. Upon being pre-

Sally Braby

Sam Carritt

Bonnie Palmer

William Bartlett

Luke Maples

sented with his prize, Luke wrecks everything by lying on his back to be tickled, his automatic reaction to most situations.

Although not a Shagpile, Cindy Harris, an extremely pretty cross between a Griffin and a Jack Russell also triumphs in the show ring. Whenever she enters she wins prizes for her excellent condition, diminutive and appealing appearance, and because the judge always wants to take her home.

'It makes a nice day out,' explains her mistress, 'and gives our mongrels a rare chance to show off.'

Cindy Harris

Cindy's looks are faintly old-fashioned. She looks a bit like an illustration in an Edwardian children's book. The exquisitely beautiful Shandy Bishop, rescued three years ago from Bath Dogs' Home, is another old-fashioned looking dog and the only mongrel to have the distinction of being photographed by that immortalizer of breed dogs, Thomas Fall. One has the feeling that Shandy would certainly have cornered all the prizes for most appealing dog before and after the Second World War, when smooth white Fox Terriers were so fashionable.

Edwina Pointon-Taylor

Bonnie Palmer, another grey Shagpile and, like Shandy Bishop, also rescued from Bath Dogs' Home, wins prizes the length and breadth of Wiltshire. The only problem of owning such a beautiful mongrel is that people keep asking what breed she is. Bonnie's owners reply that she's a 'Wiltshire Hound', which seems to keep most people quiet.

Edwina Pointon-Taylor of Beaconsfield has the same problem. A charming Black and Tan Tightskin found stranded on an island in the Thames, she has now moved to Buckinghamshire, an area so infested with dog snobs that her owner now describes her as a 'Chiltern Cheesehound'. To one dog snob he added the information that Edwina was descended from this ancient breed which used to smell out cheese when it was smuggled across the Chilterns to avoid the customs tariffs between Oxford and Buckinghamshire – hence her long nose and turn of speed. Some time later, Edwina's owner bumped into the snob's husband.

Shandy Bishop

'Linda's not speaking to you,' he said reprovingly. 'She sat up half the night trying to look up Chiltern Cheesehounds.'

In the same vein, Judy Campbell was so beautiful that everyone inquired into her pedigree. Eventually her mistress decided it would be less embarrassing for Judy if she had one, so she became the first Marsh Hatchett Hound. It was unfortunate that an uncle who'd fallen for Judy rang up Harrods and ordered one of the breed. He didn't forgive the Campbells for some years.

Judy Campbell

Chapter 20

The mongrel athlete

Few new sports have charmed the public more over the last few years than dog show jumping which is now often slotted into the middle of horse or pedigree-dog shows to give the crowd some much needed light relief. Unlike horses, the dogs seem to enjoy themselves tremendously as they wriggle along rubber tunnels, bound through hoops, sit quivering for ten seconds in a marked square, and follow their galloping owner over a series of jumps. If the owner is young, pretty and well endowed, the crowd get double the pleasure. Happily too this is one canine sporting contest which welcomes mongrels as well as breed dogs. At the Dunhill show at Olympia at Christmas 1980, Border Collies bagged first and second place in the finals, with an Alsatian (rescued from Battersea) coming third. By far the most popular dog with the crowd however was a mongrel from Crick, Northampton, called 'The Tyke'. A jaunty black and white Borderline Collie, she was sadly beaten into fourth place. Her popularity however grew to such an extent as she worked her way (barking noisily) through the heats that the BBC wired her mistress, Mrs Ashby, up for sound so that her breathless cajolements and exhortations could be heard by every one.

Tyke herself is nearly four years old. A born show-off, she thoroughly enjoyed Olympia and became more and more excited with each performance. At home, as befits a great athlete, she has an excellent appetite apart from a regrettable penchant for potato peelings. If she's given a marrow-bone she buries it immediately, and if she can't get into the garden she will hide it under a cushion or even a pillow.

Other sporting activities include playing swingball in the garden, bouncing balloons in the air for hours on end until they finally hit the ground, when she bursts them, and trying to catch seagulls on the beach. She also swims after the family rowing boat, clambering in with help and then shaking herself

Tyke and Zade Ashby

all over the occupants, and plays tug-of-war with Zade, the Ashby's other Borderline Collie. Zade also pulls Christmas crackers.

The only thing that really upset Tyke at Olympia was the firing of the Royal Artillery cannons in the final parade. She had to be given three balloons of her own to burst to keep her mind off the din.

Many owners, of course, believe that in the event of a dog Olympics their dog would qualify for a medal. Brandy Seymour of Hillingdon, a Spanish Policeman's Hat Ear Dog, seems convinced he's a horse, and always clears every fence by inches at the local gymkhana. Patch Mills, a Borderline Collie appropriately from Bath, is such a keen swimmer that he spends three-quarters of an hour every day training in the river, twisting, turning and swimming under water, and tossing the spray in his face. Most mongrels, however, need an incentive to spur them on to athletic endeavour. Teddy Billinger, yet another Borderline Collie, so hated to be left at home that when his mistress set off in the car he would race after her at 30 m.p.h. invariably catching up and being given a ride. My own Mabel can climb twelve feet up a tree, but only after squirrels or cats. While Biggles Deane, a chestnut brown rough-haired Fox Dog, can leap seven feet in the air, but only after a held-up ball.

Biggles Deane

Other mongrels excel at ball games. Ben Goundrill, a Bertrand Russell, so adored cricket that he used to dominate the children's games. This went so far that his mistress kept hearing cries from the garden of, 'It's not *fair*, you've got Ben on your side.' To keep the peace, Mrs Goundrill used to lock Ben in the attic, but he always escaped, sliding down the roof, jumping the rest of the way, and then rushing back to the cricket field. No damage was done: he lived to be nineteen.

Tess Blackburn, the Rough Diamond and aeroplane chaser, is another ballaholic. 'She even goes to sleep with a ball in her mouth,' writes her mistress. 'She owns about six. In the main she prefers men as they throw a better ball. If the gardener won't spend the afternoon throwing her ball for her, she carefully places it in front of his mowing machine.'

Other mongrels are less self-centred. Pippa Woodbridge, the white Bertrand Russell who detests late nights, will always ballboy for her mistress when she plays tennis. And Oswald Saunders, a magnificently stalwart black and tan Prop Forward, cheerfully tows two not-so-small boys on their roller skates round Sidcup every morning.

Oswald Saunders

Patch Gill of Burnley, an extremely handsome Standard

168

Magpie, was the only dog allowed into the enclosure when his master was bowling. He never went on the grass, but would sit on the path and, as soon as he saw where Mr Gill was sending his bowls, would walk round and sit there watching.

Patch Gill

One of the most impressive dog athletes must be Boot McWilliams, a grey and white General Wolfehound, who left the somewhat cramped conditions of Battersea Dogs' Home and immediately embarked on a marathon 550-mile walking tour round Somerset, Minehead and Poole. With true mongrel stamina and loyalty he never once lagged behind, coping easily with the scheduled fifteen miles a day and simultaneously forging a marvellous relationship with his new mistress. This Boot was obviously made for walking.

Pal King, a sixteen-year-old miniature Prop Forward from Doncaster, always goes coarse fishing with his master and waits 200 yards down the river. At the cry of 'Daddy's got a fish,' Pal races back, wades into the water chest-high, and brings the fish in gently in his mouth. The vet told Mr King, 'I can see Pal's very clever by his head.'

Boot McWilliams

Doris Potter, the spectacular Satin Crammer from Iver who once walked the length of the table in the middle of a dinner party, is also a keen supporter of four-course fishing. As soon as the season begins, all the fishermen take up their positions under huge green umbrellas along the lake behind her house. The moment they are concentrating on their fish, Doris advances stealthily from behind and helps herself liberally from their sandwich boxes. To add variety to her diet she has been known to gobble up the ancient mildewed kippers they used as bait.

Like most humans, mongrels tend to disapprove of blood sports until they get the opportunity to indulge in them. Rikki Bruce-Lockhart, formerly of Spain and now of Barnes, once attended a very smart grouse shoot in Scotland – strictly as a spectator. He was bored to death until suddenly he spied a mountain hare and gave noisy chase, whereupon all the other normally well disciplined gun dogs abandoned their posts and joined in. Forthwith Rikki was banned from taking part in any sporting occasion.

Pal King

Missy Ingrams, a fine Jack Russell from Aldworth prefers to do her own hunting, and despite the shouts of her owners disappears down the road in a puff of smoke in pursuit of any living thing. Deaf to all entreaty, she also vanishes down foxholes for hours at a time. Lucky Haran, an incredibly patrician-looking Ebony Fetcher, with a pedigree incestuous enough for

169

any breed dog, also lets the side down by absolutely loathing all water: the only time she was taken duck shooting she ran a mile.

On the other hand Lassie Clare, a Family Circler, was a marvellous gun dog. Her only fault was that she used to get absolutely furious with her master if he missed anything.

My own three dogs love hunting and become even more ungovernable than usual during the voling season (1 January to 31 December) when they plug their heads into vole holes with fearful snorts and take it in turns to scrabble frantically. Fortnum generally digs the vole out; Mabel, the kindest, kills it with one swift crunch of her jaws, and Barbara, unless checked, sucks it in like spaghetti, devouring fur, tail and all in one swallow. This and squirrelling apart, their sole athletic achievement is restricted to Fortnum once winning the Putney Common Association mothers' race, for which he was awarded an ice cream.

Chapter 21

The mongrel and the arts

One seldom touched-on aspect of the mongrel character is their keen appreciation of the arts. Many of them, for example, have a very good ear for music. In her excellent history of Battersea Dogs' Home, Lady Cottesloe tells the story of a little dog of very mixed origin who went to live with a pianist and promptly restricted him in the music he played. The dog adored Chopin and would listen to a ballade or a nocturne with a silly besotted grin on its face. At the first few bars of Liszt, however, it would flee howling from the room. Benjy Cowen, an Old Sea Dog from Newcastle, hates pop music but has a passion for Wagner.

Other mongrels are born with fine singing voices. Bob Follows, a Rough Diamond from Walsall, had the most amazing range covering several octaves. The moment the mouth organ was fetched he would sit up and join in, following the music with a series of tuneful howls ranging from a deep rumbling growl to a high pitched whine. Similarly Nobby Kempster of Warrington, a slim Prop Forward with a badger stripe down his forehead, was very good at hitting the right notes, singing together with his mistress, and even changing key. He also liked Kathleen Ferrier, and if one of her records was played on the wireless, would sit down in front of the set and join in.

Bob Follows

Nobby Kempster

Boris Jones (named after Boris Godunov), a splendid black General Wolfehound with a very Russian white-flecked beard, was also an excellent singer, 'I was born under a wandering star' being his star turn. On the strength of this he was asked to join a singing group for their annual concert. Alas, poor Boris got terrible stage fright on the night, refused to sing in front of the audience, and retired from public life, with his career in smithereens.

Some dogs have the star quality without the talent. Simba O'Donohue of Inishowen, a Borderline Collie with a sprinkling of tan around the face, was a great exhibitionist.

173

Boris Jones

Leo Lewis-Bowen

Pongo Cubey

'If we had a party at home, 'writes his mistress, 'and guests were applauding for a song or dance, Simba believed the applause was for him. He promptly took the centre of the floor, chasing his tail with gusto, and always stealing the limelight.'

Nor does Leo Lewis-Bowen display much reticence either. A remarkable Great Dane/Dachshund cross, he loves music and will accompany any singer, especially a contralto. His most hilarious escapade was when the Women's Institute held a meeting at Mrs Lewis-Bowen's house. They kicked off as usual with 'Jerusalem', but the hymn was never completed as Leo placed himself in the middle of the singers and joined in so heartily that no one else could carry on.

Little Pongo Cubey, a Family Circler with vast appealing eyes, came from a petshop window in Camden Town. As there had been a travelling circus in the area a few weeks before, her owners were convinced she had been left behind by them, or was at least the result of a brief coupling between a circus dog and one of the local bitches. Apart from the many tricks she picked up instantly, she had a natural sense of rhythm. Top of the hit parade at the time was 'How Much is that Doggie in the Window? (*woof, woof*), The one with the waggly tail (*woof, woof*).' Owing to the circumstances in which they acquired Pongo, the Cubeys started to sing this song to her. Immediately, she started to bark in accompaniment to the '*woof, woof*s,' not only when her owners sang the words, but also if they recited them on one note or merely hummed the tune.

The late Many Esdaile, a merry white Bertrand Russell with brown patches, showed such talent for accompanying the piano that his master wrote him a special signature tune. As soon as it was played on the piano, Many would rush in from the garden and joyfully give tongue. He obviously approved of signature tunes, because the music that introduced 'Radio Newsreel' on the Home Service produced the same result.

I have received numerous letters from owners describing their dog's reaction to music on television. The dog Seeley, a Standard Magpie from Suffolk, always barks with joy when he hears the music at the end of *Crossroads*, knowing it is the cue for his owners to get up and take him out. On the other hand Chuffy Hopkins, a Cairn cross from Stockport, is allergic to the signature tune of *Coronation Street* and goes berserk when she hears it, leaping at the television and barking like mad. No other tune affects her in this way. Heidi Southworth, the original Ear Commodore from Radcliffe, Manchester, is even more particular; not only *Coronation Street* music, but the signature tunes of

174

Tomorrow's World, Nationwide, ITV News and *Match of the Day* trigger off the most despairing and disapproving wails. While Tessie and Judy Jupp, a Shagpile and a Family Circler from Ilford, don't mind signature tunes but can't stand the quavering sopranos in old musical films, and put back their heads and howl until the television is turned off.

Barney Leete-Hodge, a Jack Russell, has equally strong views on music on television. He enjoys country-and-western and folk music, but can't stand opera, stalking out of the room and sitting halfway up the stairs like a Grand Old Duke of York until the last act is over. He also hates jazz. Gyp Whittaker goes even further. If he can't stand a television programme he can change Channels with his nose.

Tim Jowett, an enchanting little Rough Diamond with a touch of shaggy Collie, also provided ample proof that mongrels recognize a particular tune when they hear it, and are not simply reacting because the tune is the cue for some pleasant or unpleasant event. During the fifties, 'Silent Night' was extremely popular with visiting carol singers. As soon as this tune floated over the cold night air, Tim would rush to the front door, barking madly until the last verse was finished. Other carols left him unmoved. He even started barking when the Beverley sisters sang 'Silent Night' on television. His owners could never work out whether he was joining in or trying to shout down the singers.

On the odd occasion when I've appeared on television or spoken on the wireless, my three dogs have displayed no interest at all – probably showing their good taste. Like many other mongrels they don't even lift their heads when a dog barks on the box. Shandy Durk, a Rough Diamond, on the other hand barked furiously whenever a dog appeared on the screen. As soon as it went off she would rush to the French windows to see where the wretched creature had gone. Tramp Trickey, the Borderline Collie who always guarded grand-children on holiday, is obviously interested in his relations, because he always watches closely when the sheepdogs appear in *One Man and His Dog*. While Tessa Bridge, a Persil-washed black and white Twentieth Century Fox Dog whose favourite sport is having a ball thrown for her, is glued to the television during golf, cricket and football programmes.

There is also another very funny story about Tim Jowett, the Rough Diamond who reacted so violently to 'Silent Night'. He was once asleep in the drawing-room when Philip Harben was showing viewers how to make a cake on television. The

Many Esdaile

Tim Jowett

Shandy Durk

moment Philip began to mix up the ingredients, banging his spoon on the bowl, Tim woke up. Looking frantically round the room he eventually spotted Philip busily stirring, and sat down absolutely riveted to the screen. Having completed that part of the recipe, Philip turned round to put the bowl down behind him. Quick as a flash Tim was round the back of the television sniffing all over the floor for the bowl he was convinced was meant for him.

The most dramatic effect on the dog-watching population for years, however, has been caused by Mrs Barbara Woodhouse. One bark of command from her sends my anarchic dogs scuttling out of the room. Similarly Sam Tomsett, a Jack Russell/ Alsatian cross from Hertford, detests Mrs Woodhouse and growls when she speaks sharply to any of the dogs on television. Harriet Jones, an adorable Satin Crammer who likes a quiet life at any price, hid under the kitchen table for the entire duration of each programme. 'She used,' said her owner, 'to be rather good at obeying when you told her to sit; now she just runs away.'

On the credit side, however, Suzie Buttling of Clwyd, another Satin Crammer, seems to have become much more obedient since watching Mrs Woodhouse, and Brandy and Sherry Holden, two Rough Diamonds, are both vastly intrigued by the programme, sitting when Mrs W. tells them to sit, and barking at all the dogs they dislike.

One of the funniest things I ever saw on television was the *Jim'll Fix It* programme in which a little girl brought her mongrel Blackie, a marvellous great shaggy tank of a General Wolfe-hound, into the studio and asked Mrs Woodhouse to suggest what his ancestry might be. Blackie was not amused, and rumbled ominously at Mrs W. when she tried to straighten his legs and make him stand up like a show dog. She then introduced various pedigree dogs who might have been part of his make-up. They included, among others, a Dachshund, a Corgi, an Airedale and a Scottie. Blackie growled furiously at all of them, and when Mrs Woodhouse suggested he should be walked round the studio on a tour of these possible relations, he nearly took a bite out of each one. She then gave up and confessed with great charm that he probably had hundreds of different breeds in his make-up. Blackie heaved a sigh of relief and was awarded his *Jim'll Fix It* medal.

In the field of literature mongrels are also significant. They may not be able to write yet, but they have inspired many writers – not altogether favourably one must confess. Even in

Homer they play a leading role, sharing with vultures the unsavoury task of scavenging. Shakespeare clearly disliked all dogs. But when he listed them in *King Lear*, only mongrels were singled out by an unflattering epithet:

> Mastiff, greyhound, mongrel *grim*,
> Hound or spaniel, brach or lym
> or bobtail tike, or trundle-tail.

Goldsmith, at least, improved matters by making the distinction between mongrels and 'curs of low degree' in his *Elegy on the Death of a Mad Dog*, and William Cowper did even better by writing magically about a mongrel enjoying a walk on a winter morning:

> Forth goes the woodman, leaving unconcerned
> The cheerful haunts of man, to wield the axe
> And drive the wedge in yonder forest drear,
> From morn to eve his solitary task.
> Shaggy, and lean, and shrewd, with pointed ears
> And tail cropp'd short, half lurcher and half cur,
> His dog attends him. Close behind his heel,
> Now creeps he slow; and now with many a frisk
> Wide scampering, snatches up the drifted snow
> With ivory teeth, or ploughs it with his snout;
> Then shakes his powder'd coat and barks for joy.

Hugh Walpole, as I mentioned earlier, was the first writer to really appreciate the rescued mongrel. Hamlet, in the *Jeremy and Hamlet* stories, was based on a real dog Walpole rescued in Great Portland Street. He saw a ruffian kicking something, and goes on:

I heard that 'something' give a shrill squeal; I crossed and discovered a very small, dirty, bleeding and dishevelled puppy. Raging as though I were myself the puppy, I abused the ruffian whereat he laughed and said I could have the perishing dog if I so wished. The 'perishing dog' was Hamlet. He was exactly as is described in the Jeremy books. He lived with me for ten years in Polperro in Cornwall, and died during the war of an incurable eczema caught from his obstinate and greedy feeding on unsavoury fish.

Many painters have been dog lovers. Perhaps, like writers, they find that mongrel companionship, unconversational but steadfast, helps to lessen the essential loneliness of their task. Janet Ledger owns a beautiful black Satin Crammer called Simon, who shadows her all day whether she is painting or doing housework. As a reward, he has appeared in many of her paintings, including two lithographs hanging in the Tate.

Cartoonist Jack Fish was also devoted to a shaggy white Bertrand Russell called Bill, who belonged to his family when he was a boy before the Second World War.

'Bill was utterly loyal and the best friend I have had,' writes Mr Fish. 'Heartbroken when he was put down in 1939, I swore if ever I got the chance I would make him famous. In 1948 I began drawing a weekly cartoon for the *Gloucestershire Echo*, one each week and still going strong. In every cartoon I included old Bill, who has now appeared more than 1,700 times. I understand readers of the paper look for him more than the implication of the cartoon.'

Numerous mongrels have appeared in films, of course, and acted both grownups and children off the screen. Some years ago Dolores, a Battersea mongrel, bagged a coveted role, starring opposite Rod Steiger in Graham Greene's *Across the Bridge*. She got marvellous notices. Here is one from the News Chronicle:

> The latest portrait in Rod Steiger's small but unforgettable rogues' gallery is the fugitive crook financier of *Across the Bridge*. You may gauge the portrait's brilliance by the fact that its perpetrator just succeeds in stealing the picture from one of the most endearing bitches in screen history.

The most celebrated mongrel Thespian, however, must be Dougal, the black Romney Marshall belonging to actor David King. He first met his master fourteen years ago, when David was acting in a play at the Haymarket Theatre and thinking of getting a dog – a pedigree one of course. One of the actresses in the cast, however, was looking for a home for Dougal, who was already on his fourth home in five months because of his tendency to rip people's places apart. Dougal and David took to each other instantly, and after a chaotic journey home on the tube (not the easiest place to carry an exuberant puppy) Dougal settled in beautifully. He proved the perfect dog for an actor; not only was he very adaptable, curling up quietly in David's dressing-room during performances, but he was also soon swelling the family coffers by acting himself. His greatest triumph was appearing at the Ludlow Festival as Moonshine's dog in *Midsummer Night's Dream*. After the last performance all the women in the play received bouquets, but his master had to get a wheel-barrow to carry away Dougal's present, which included a large bar of chocolate and three enormous shin bones.

When his master was acting in *Henry IV* at the Ludlow Festival, however, there was no part for Dougal. One evening he got bored with sitting in the dressing-room and wandered off. Just as Glendower was making his famous boast about being a magician and calling spirits from the vasty deep, to the horror of the actors but the delighted surprise of the audience, on trotted Dougal. He had a quick sniff round the stage, and, not finding anything interesting, disappeared into the wings again.

I first met Dougal some years ago when I wrote a piece about the Christmas performance of *Toad of Toad Hall* for the *Sunday Times*. David, his master, was playing Badger, a part he's taken every year since 1952. Dougal was appearing as the Nanny's dog, putting in a brief but telling appearance at the beginning of the play, and then spending the rest of the performance trying to mount the back leg of the barge horse.

Apart from acting in *Toad* for the last seven years, and having his story told by his master on *Jackanory*, Dougal also appeared as the farmer's dog in a performance of Chekov's *The Proposal*. Evidently he was brilliant in rehearsal, settling down on the carpet, rolling over on his back, and scratching his nose with his paws in the most realistic way. When he came on at the actual performance, however, all the audience said 'aaaaaah'. Being a courteous dog, Dougal went to have a closer look at them, and seeing several of his master's friends jumped off the stage and sat down beside them, leaving the actors to get on with the play as best they could.

Dougal's career in films has been less successful, simply because he doesn't believe in working without an audience. When playing an old tramp in *Z Cars* on location, he refused to act at all until some children came out of a nearby school at 3.30 and walked home past the set. Immediately he realized he was

179

Dougal and David King

being admired, Dougal rose to the occasion and put on a brilliant performance.

Like most prima doggas, Dougal doesn't like competition. While his master was acting at the Birmingham Repertory Theatre for a year, he had to share a dressing-room with two Labradors, and sulked terribly. He was even more put out that

180

Christmas when he appeared in *Treasure Island* and discovered the parrot had a much bigger part than he did. Despite having reservations about other livestock, however, he is unfailingly courteous to human members of the cast. When appearing in pantomime in Worthing, he always stood aside for the Principal Boy on the stairs.

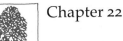

Chapter 22

The dogs of war

*But of all the world's brave heroes, there's none that can
compare with the bow, wow, wow, wow, wow, wow,
wow, of the British mongrel cur*

Nowhere do mongrels show up to greater advantage than in
war. One thinks not only of the valour which enabled them to
bag six out of the sixteen dog VCs issued in the Second World
War, but also of the way they remain cheerful under the most
horrific circumstances.

To examine their valour first, we must start at the beginning
of the Second World War when the public were invited to lend
their dogs for the war effort. Well aware how devoted the British
are to their animals, the War Office was pessimistic about the
response and laid on a skeleton staff. Within a few days this staff
was buckling under offers from more than 7,000 owners, asking
only that their beloved animal should be given the chance to
prove its worth.

Among many heartbreaking letters was one which said, 'My
husband has gone, my son has gone, please take my dog to
bring this cruel war to an end.'

Not many of the dogs submitted were suitable. They needed a
sanguine temperament and a keen sense of smell. Mongrels
were avoided on the whole because of the usual argument that
they were unpredictable. The ones that did get through all
looked vaguely like breed dogs. A good example was a Family
Circler of exceptional courage called Bob. After his training, he
was attached to 'C' Company of the 6th Royal West Kents and
went with the regiment to North Africa where he excelled at
carrying messages, guarding stores, and accompanying recce
patrols. Bob won his Dickin Medal (the dogs' Victoria Cross) at
Green Hill, when with his white patches camouflaged with dark
paint he led a night patrol into enemy lines. Suddenly he froze

in his tracks. The patrol waited, and then, seeing nothing ahead, ignored the dog's warning and decided to push on. Bob refused to budge. Next second movement was discerned in the faint light 200 yards ahead. Bob had saved the patrol from almost certain capture or death.

This gallant mongrel went right through the Sicilian and Italian campaigns, and in cold weather wore a warm coat embroidered with the regimental crest. Tragically, while being retired to England to be re-united with his demobbed master, Bob slipped his collar in Milan and was never seen again.

Rob, another patrol mongrel who also won a Dickin Medal, happily survived to receive it and thoroughly enjoyed being mobbed like a Beatle at the ceremony. A glorious grinning Borderline Collie with a large black patch over one eye, he served with the SAS and took part in landings in North Africa with the infantry unit, and then served with them again in Italy. Most of the work was extremely dangerous. Known as the 'Paradog', he made over twenty parachute landings, and guarded small parties exploring enemy territory. Like Bob, Rob saved numerous lives.

Brian

A third Dickin Medal was deservedly won by an Alsatian cross called Brian, who served in the 13th Battalion Airborne Division. Landing in Normandy, he did enough drops to become a qualified parachutist. In his official photograph Brian is shown with his head cocked on one side. Rather like American soldiers in films who always wear their peaked caps at a raffish un-English angle, he exudes a jolly chocolate-boxy charm which would never be seen in a pure breed Alsatian.

Some of the brightest and best dogs lent to the War Office were allotted to the unenviable task of detecting mines and, in Holland alone, checked nearly 100 miles of railway line. Dogs were trained to sit down the instant they picked up the smell of a mine, and with luck this was a few yards short of the danger spot. Quite one of the bravest mine dogs was a beautiful Shagpile called Rickie, described rather evasively in the official reports as 'a short-legged Welsh Sheepdog'. After a training course he served in France, Belgium and Holland. He was clearing a canal bank in Holland when in the middle of the exercise one of the mines, though detected, blew up, killing the section commander and wounding Rickie in the face. With remarkable heroism, he remained calm and continued his task of detecting further mines, winning himself a Dickin Medal in the process. The experience seems to have taken its toll. In the photograph, Rickie's eyes stare out, wistful and haunted, through his long fringe of hair.

Rickie

184

Bitches figure less frequently on the Roll of Honour, but no one could deny the courage of a mongrel bitch called Gypsy, who moved south with her master for the invasion of Normandy and then accompanied him across the channel, nonchalantly having two puppies on the high seas. Like Rickie she travelled through France, Belgium and Holland, then on to Luxembourg and Germany. Officially recognized by the Dutch Government as the first English dog over the Rhine and Elbe rivers, she was presented with an engraved collar (and presumably a good dinner) at the Continental Restaurant in Brussels. Later, sadly, this affectionate, charming dog was wounded in an air-raid during the Ardennes push, spent six weeks in plaster, and was left lame in one leg and, even worse for a dog, with a paralysed tail, so there was no wagging when peace was declared.

The Dickin Medal, donated by the People's Dispensary for Sick Animals, is engraved with the words, 'For gallantry – we also serve.' The colours of the ribbon are green, brown and pale blue to symbolize valour on sea, land and in the sky. It was first awarded during the Second World War, but there is no doubt it would have been won by Sammy, a ginger Bertrand Russell, who was one of the most courageous participants in the First World War. As mascot of the Royal Northumberland Fusiliers, Sammy went to France with the regiment in 1915, was wounded in the second battle of Ypres, gassed on Whit Monday and burned by shell fire on several occasions, but survived and remained with his regiment during the advance on the Somme.

But perhaps the most famous of all military mongrels was Bobbie, a pale Golden Fetcher with strange Asiatic eyes. Having survived the battle of Maiwand, where he was wounded, and achieved immortality by his inclusion in the famous painting of that encounter called 'The Last Eleven', he returned to England. He was personally decorated by Queen Victoria for his bravery and somewhat incongruously met his end under the wheels of a hansom cab in Gosport. Queen Victoria is said to have cried when she heard this sad news.

Repeatedly impressive is the cheerful stoicism with which the mongrel endures pain. One of the most touching photographs from the First World War is of a huge shaggy messenger dog, a General Wolfehound, with all four paws bandaged because of agonizing mustard gas burns, but still managing to grin at the cameraman.

It is also remarkable, bearing in mind the usual mongrel devotion to his owner, how in war he is able to adjust to different

185

BOBBIE (Owned by Sergt P. Kelly) Pet of the 66th. Survived the Afghan Campaign 1879 & 1880. Was wounded at Maiwand 27th July 1880. Came home with the Battalion Feb 1881, & was decorated with the Afghan Medal by Her Majesty the Queen, at Osborne, June 1881. Was accidently killed at Gosport, Oct 13, 1882.

owners. One thinks of Rats (*see* p. 182), the little Ear Commodore, who served so long and gamely in Northern Ireland. Attached to the Queen's Own Highlanders, then to the Welsh Guards, he went on ceaseless patrols, helicopter flights, and car chases with a string of different masters. Finally these exertions took their toll of his small frame. On doctor's orders, Rats was ordered to rest. Happily he was given an honourable retirement. A dog-loving friend of the regiment offered him a home in the country in Kent. According to his new master, Rats adjusted to civilian life, 'as only a mongrel could'. Having lived in army quarters for eight years, he had never been housetrained or met a woman before. In a few days, he was quite clean in the house, and, to his master's slight jealousy, was curling up ecstatically every night on his mistress's lap. New hobbies, taken up with alacrity, include chasing the local pheasants and writing his autobiography shortly to be published.

Another unselfish, adaptable mongrel, in the last war was a black and white Terrier called Sam who was attached to the Royal Engineers and had to remain with the corps when his beloved master was invalided back to England. Unflinchingly he travelled with them through Italy, Belgium and Germany, was present at the invasion of Salerno, and triumphantly entered Naples barking noisily on the bonnet of an armoured car. According to the official handout he was 'very popular, and loved by everyone in his unit.'

No one should doubt either that the Germans loved their dogs of war as much as the British. Another very moving First World War photograph shows a German messenger dog delivering grenades to a handful of men under fire in a shell hole. The soldier who is removing the grenades from the dog's carrier bag is bending over the animal, sheltering him fleetingly with his body while the dog's head is pressed lovingly against the soldier's breast.

One heartrending photograph also shows a German Rough Diamond being taken prisoner at the Battle of Passchendaele. The dog's lead, twisted up like barley sugar, tells us how hard he must have struggled to escape. Now he limps along, dejection in every inch of his drenched rough coat. But perhaps a new bond is forming, for to his left a smiling English soldier in a tin hat stretches out a tentative hand to touch him.

The dog in fact is one of the few casualties of war who often passes safely and happily into enemy hands. Sappho, a black mongrel, started her career in the Second World War on a German flak ship, but when it was captured at Porte en Bessin

187

Sammy, mascot of the Northumberland Fusiliers, wounded at Ypres and survived the advance on the Somme

German dog being taken prisoner – October 1917

A mongrel entertains American, French and British sailors at Trouville, August 1918

The mongrel gets a lift – the Amiens-Albert Road, 25th August, 1916

Rip rescues a victim in the Blitz

on D-Day she transferred very happily to *HMS Ursa* as their mascot.

Many poor Dachshunds were stoned in the streets in England during the First World War because of their German origins. Tocra, a little Daxi cross, fared better however. Formerly a mascot of a Panzer division, she was picked up as a terrified stray in Tocra, near Benghazi, and adopted by a unit of the Royal Signals. Attaching herself instantly to one of the soldiers, she became a complete one-man bitch. On the eve of the Battle of Mareth she produced six puppies, all of whom died. Then after numerous adventures in Africa she made a long sea voyage home, and, when the unit was sent to France, was left in England to await her new master's return at the end of the war.

In war, as in peace, the rescued mongrel displays unshakable loyalty to the person who saves it. Tich, another stray, who was found in Egypt, a country not noted for its courage, became the mascot of the first battalion of the King's Royal Rifle Corps in Italy and North Africa, and went into action with her new master, Rifleman Walker, trailing him wherever he went. To his intense pride and delight she was awarded the Dickin Medal for 'loyalty, courage and devotion under hazardous conditions of war from 1941–45.'

Benghazi obviously yields up curs of character. Yet another stray only a few days old was dug out of the rubble of a bombed-out house during the advance at El Alamein. Re-christened 'Benghazi Ben' he became the mascot of the RASC, travelling through Libya, Tripolitania, Tunisia and Egypt, often riding on the roof of the cab of a lorry. What impressed the men was Ben's total fearlessness under fire. When he was run over the whole unit mourned him. He was buried in the desert with full military honours, and inscribed on the PDSA Roll of Honour.

Time and again one notices in war how a shivering, terrified dog becomes as brave as a lion once he finds a master to love and to guard. Peter, a panic-stricken stray picked up from bombed rubble in Normandy by men from the Royal Signals, soon became almost blasé about shell and gun fire. It was noticed, however, that he learnt to anticipate the approach of shells and always took cover. While Flash, the offspring of an Irish Terrier crossed with a Whippet (not the most courageous of breeds) went overseas with the 61st Field Regiment to Normandy, survived the battles of Caen, Villiers Bocages and Falaise, and made herself extremely useful catching hares and rabbits for the pot during fighting on the front line.

The mongrel's most important military function, however, is

to provide light relief. Flip through the huge photograph albums of the Imperial War Museum, and sooner or later you will find a little dog not doing anything heroic but just injecting a welcome note of comedy into the grim opera of war. There are pictures of mongrels in gas-masks, or grinning in sailor hats, or begging for pieces of chocolate in the trenches, or sitting on top of a piano in the debris of a bombed city, the yapping centre of an impromptu sing-song. Mongrels too seem to appeal to all ranks. One of my favourite Imperial War Museum photographs, taken in August 1916, shows a handsome, beautifully turned-out officer strolling along the Amiens–Albert Road past a field of equally well turned out corn stooks. He is leading his horse on which proudly rides a little Miniature Magpie. Another favourite, taken towards the end of the war, shows a group of exhausted soldiers collapsed for a moment's respite in the ruins of a bombed house. One of them, like a child cuddling a teddy bear, holds a white mongrel in his arms; the dog's head rests on his shoulder with a look of infinite trust on its face. For men so far from home, lonely, frightened, under constant threat of death and deprived of family or girlfriends, a dog which could unstintingly receive and return affection must have provided immeasurable solace.

Thus, amongst the unsung heroes of war have been all those mascot mongrels who without doing anything particularly gallant kept up everyone's spirits: Sally, for example, attached to the RASC, flew 15,000 miles in a DC3 and was described in the official reports as 'very popular with all members of the unit'; or Tiffany, a black-and-white mongrel bitch, mascot of the RAC, who 'learnt several tricks and provided the men with much amusement'.

The value of this ability to keep smiling was nobly demonstrated by Peggy, a shaggy mongrel, and Simon, a black-and-white cat, who were living on *HMS Amethyst* when she was bombarded by Chinese Communists in the Yangtze river in 1947. Simon was badly wounded by a shell, but carried on ratting after the bombardment and was awarded a Dickin Medal. Both Simon and Peggy, according to the official report, 'were decisive factors in maintaining a high level of morale among the ship's company and helped to impart an air of normality during the trying period after bombardment.' They also serve who only stand and woof.

Sandy, another most endearing ginger Bertrand Russell, served in the Royal Navy base at Rosyth. The names of his ships, which included *Hercules, New Zealand, Lion* and the *Ark*

190

Royal, were engraved on a smart brass plaque on his collar. One sailor, Mr Jenner, remembers joining the *Ark Royal* and meeting Sandy in 1922 when the ship was still in Turkish waters because the Turks still hadn't signed the peace treaty. Sandy obviously had a bitch in every port, for whenever liberty men went ashore he was the first to land, scampering off on his own. Although unsupervised, he always knew with true mongrel foresight when the ship was about to sail, and would be waiting on the jetty.

Sandy

Back on the home front, there are numerous tales of mongrel heroism. *Esprit de cur* was perhaps best epitomized by Ben, the mascot of the National Fire Brigade during the frantic days of the Blitz and later during the 'doodlebug' raids. Described by the chief fireman as a 'regular little cockney, sharp as a needle', Ben would jump on the first fire engine to go out, when the alarm bells rang. He would climb up the ladder with the men, and went to every fire with them, not getting in their way, but fiercely watching every move as he guarded the pumps in the streets.

Another mongrel hero, whose indefatigable service won him a Dickin Medal, was a black and tan Ear Commodore called Rip. In appearance very much like Rats from Northern Ireland, he was found homeless and hungry after a heavy raid in September 1940. Rip then turned rescue dog himself and was given the official job of locating people trapped under bombed buildings. How welcome to the victims must have been the sound of those scrabbling paws and Terrier yelps, and the first sight of that grinning Tommy Brock face with its merry friendly eyes and white moustache. Mascot of the ARP at Poplar, Rip saved numerous lives and was adored by everyone who met him, particularly children.

One letter which particularly moved me while I was writing this book came from a Mrs Day of Southport, who remembers in 1944 when she was only eight years old her parents' house receiving a direct hit from a flying bomb. Nine houses in the street were flattened and twenty-two people killed. Of her family, only Mrs Day and her father survived.

'Dad,' she writes, 'was trapped under the rubble and called to the rescuers to dig underneath him as he thought a child was buried there. They dug and dug, and suddenly out jumped our mongrel Kerry, who bolted, though obviously injured. I was taken to hospital and lay in bed, day after day, worrying about my lost dog. After three weeks I was discharged from hospital and sent up to Leicester to convalesce. Badly scarred on my face

191

and legs, I was suffering far more inside from shock and grief. Just as I was walking up the platform, I saw Kerry (a neighbour had somehow traced him to Kingston). He was only a small dog, but he managed to yank himself free, and hurl himself against my chest. He couldn't stop licking my face. I boarded that train feeling nearer happiness than I thought I ever would again. Kerry saved me from losing my reason.'

Kerry, a little Lancashire Hot Pet, was lucky enough to be re-united with his mistress. Poor Mrs Stannard, like hundreds of other owners, had to part with her black and tan Terrier, Rex (who was actually a bitch), when her husband was posted to Inverness and their new landlady (also a bitch) refused to take the dog as well. In despair, Mrs Stannard asked a friend to wait until she and her husband had left for Scotland and then take Rex to be put down. Luckily, on the way to the vet Rex sat down on the pavement, and gazed up with such sad, appealing eyes that the friend decided to keep her instead. She was amply rewarded. Rex always 'barked before German planes came over and was loved by all.'

During the worst raids, another mongrel, Pat Hedges, was an enormous comfort to her deaf mistress. The moment the siren went the dog would gently wake her up, and lead her down to the shelter. Chum Scotchbrook, a handsome black Family Circler with ginger sideboards, also anticipated every raid. He would scratch at his mistress's door, and the family would then gather in the shelter. The moment they'd got settled, sure enough the siren would go. As another bonus, the family were able to go to bed before the All Clear. Chum would suddenly get up, leave the shelter, and settle down in his basket with a deep contented sigh. He was never wrong; two minutes later the All Clear would go.

One correspondent described how her brave but slightly mis-guided mongrel always rushed out and lay on top of the baby in her pram the moment the siren went. Nor did Jacky Bowyer-Kairns, a brown and white Hover Cur, need much prompting. The family cat had had kittens, and as soon as the siren went Jackie used to carry them one by one to the Anderson shelter, with the cat walking beside him mewing and supervising. Once the All Clear went, however, Jacky retired to bed and left the cat to carry her offspring back herself.

Zam Williams, a large white and brown very long-legged Bertrand Russell absolutely bristling with character, was much less altruistic but nevertheless kept everyone amused. 'In the war,' writes Mrs Williams, 'we had a table shelter in the lounge.

Zam Williams

192

Zam used to occupy most of our bed (very bad habit). As soon as the warning came, he was first down the stairs, taking up most of the shelter to continue his sleep. We had a siren opposite, and by way of a change on warm evenings he would run out and sit on the wall and howl top note. The neighbours used to laugh and say "There's Zam Williams joining in again".'

During the black-out it must have been very frightening for women to walk home alone at night. Once again mongrels came to the rescue.

'Mother ran the WVS,' writes Miss Letete-Hodge. 'Often she used to work very late. If he felt she was too late, Daddy would send Benny, our Jack Russell, to meet her. He would go unerringly to her office in the town, scratch at the door, and then walk her home, growling.'

Finally, one of the most remarkable dogs of war must be a resourceful Rough-and-Reddish called Jane.

'Her clever nose for balls,' according to her mistress Mrs Golder, 'kept my children supplied, when they were very scarce during the war. Her top total for a day's outing would be up to fourteen balls lost in the scrub or depth of bramble bushes. When the holidays were over, the children were able to supply all their friends with balls.'

Jane Golder

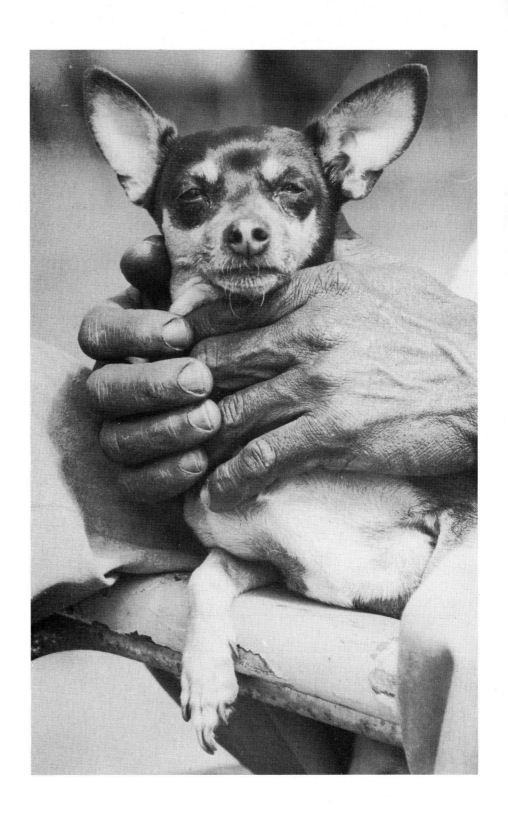

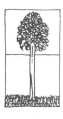

Chapter 23

The leak of nations

Noel Coward was wrong. It's not the mad dogs, but the extremely sensible ones, who go out in the mid-day sun. They know this is the time when they are most likely to meet a tender hearted female tourist who will be so outraged by their flea-infested, undernourished condition that she will promptly ply them with good food, whip them off to the nearest vet, and at vast expense take them back to the UK. Mongrels abroad often have desperately hard lives. Consequently if you befriend a foreign dog, his love and loyalty are unshakable.

A case in point is a glorious Alsatian cross called Rikki (*see p.214*) who was found in Marbella by an English girl, Tanya Bruce-Lockhart. At the time he was homeless, half-starved, with one broken leg and no hair on his head. A lady of resourcefulness, as befits a successful television director, Miss Bruce-Lockhart fed Rikki, had his leg set by a vet, took a room for him in the extremely chic and exclusive Marbella Club, and, after much argee-bargee with the Spanish authorities, had him flown back to London in a tin box. Rikki, who has now given his unstinting devotion to her for fifteen years, is estimated by the vet to be at least seventeen, and is still going strong. His many escapades include breaking up a grouse shoot, and being described by Peter Hall as an 'automated coffee table'. It is written into Miss Bruce-Lockhart's television contracts that wherever she goes Rikki goes too. On one occasion when she took him to Asprey's to buy him an evening collar, he wandered off and affectionately goosed an American lady in a mink coat.

'Oh, my Gard,' screamed the lady, 'what a hideous dog.'

'You don't look so hot yourself,' said Miss Bruce-Lockhart sweetly, 'but I'm sure you have a beautiful nature.'

Australia: Toby Munro. Old English Sheepdog crossed with Irish Wolfhound. Weighs eight stone.

Singapore: Honey Powell. Ate lizards, guarded the family from fierce snakes and always greeted her master with a frangipani flower when he came home from work.

Hong Kong: Jumble Evans. Unwanted Christmas present found abandoned with rope around his waist on Boxing Day. Despite spectacular good looks, resembles a hyena more than a dog.

Singapore: Timmy Perrin. Pye dog found in monsoon drain. Travelled to Germany, then England.

The Isle of Man: Digby Matthews. Cheats at hide-and-seek by not counting up to ten.

Germany: Brackie Leete. Found half-starved, chained to a three-sided tea chest. Rescued from cruel master and brought back to England.

Crete: Maria Cohen. Lived on top of holiday villa, indulging in noisy moonlit frolics with assorted admirers.

Malta: Tahli Giles. Found covered in sores and fleas on a rubbish dump in 1977. Now radiant and 'as plump as a rugger ball' in Hampstead.

Menorca: Rosie Richardson. Rescued and brought back to England with great difficulty. 'Why is your dog leaving Spain,' asked one Spanish official, 'does she not like it here?'

Iran: Bessie Bemrose. Spent dreadful puppyhood going from bad home to worse, living on orange peel and hiding in drains to avoid fierce packs of wild dogs. Now resides happily in Ripon, occasionally taking fourteenth place at dinner parties. Sporadic bad behaviour instantly checked if ticked off in Iranian.

Ghana: Sid Whitchurch. Tamed bushdog. Lived with five cats, waiting until they were eating dinner and then rushing at them, barking hysterically. Having scattered the cats, he would help himself to their food but, when caught in the act, would stop dead and look at his mistress with a 'stupid sort of grin on his face, wagging his tail feebly'.

Tennessee: Nipper De'Ath. Scottish Terrier cross of shaggy appearance, cylindrical body and skipping gait. Tennessee locals ask: 'Is that a dawg or a ground hawg?'

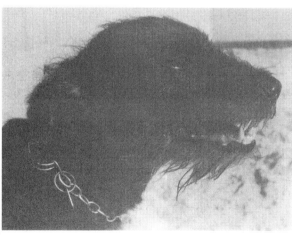

The Oman: Whiskers Pemberton. Adopted new owners by jumping into their parked car while they were admiring the view. Now much travelled around the Gulf.

America: Shamus Faber. Rescued from the Humane Society in St Louis. Date of birth unknown. Celebrates official birthday on April 1.

198

India: Whiskey Waddell. Rescued from being used as a football by a group of boys. 'With careful nursing this mangy bundle grew into a fat lovable fellow.' He liked to get his cold snout under women's dresses at dinner parties but, after a bit, they got to know him and didn't take much notice.

South Africa: Bozo Smeddle. Rescued in Cape Town. Returned to England first class on the Union Castle line while his owners went steerage, P & O.

Ceylon: Pettah Holman and son. Rescued from local bazaar, dying of mange. Taken home to be put down. Fortunately, the Matron of the local hospital was staying and completely cured Pettah by prescribing medicine normally used for scabies in humans.

Rhodesia: Frumpy Purkis. Heavy sleeper and failed guard dog. Chickens stolen three times from under her nose and several visits from intruders unheeded. Excellent swimmer.

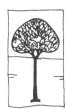

Chapter 24

Curvoyants

Many mongrels have a remarkable ability to distinguish different days of the week and others are excellent timekeepers. A dog is a creature of routine with a built-in time clock. Perhaps the same kind of instinct tells birds it is time to migrate when the days start getting shorter.

What is less easy to explain is how so many dogs anticipate the arrival of their master or mistress even when they don't turn up at a regular time. One mongrel owner in Australia, who jets around the world a great deal, said that at first her dog missed her dreadfully when she left home but after a day or two settled into a routine with the housekeeper, of whom he was very fond. Whenever his mistress returned home, however, the moment her plane landed the dog sensed it, and started screaming with excitement. He wouldn't settle until her car finally drew up at the front door.

Kim Spink of Dorking, a sleek Standard Magpie with a badger stripe down his forehead, always knew when any of the family would be coming home. They all turned up at different times of the day, and there was no routine about this, but Kim always stationed himself at the stairs window, ten minutes before each arrival.

Kim had the badger stripe which seems to be a characteristic of dogs with second sight. He also had a Borderline Collie mother, and mongrels with Collie blood also seem to be particularly psychic. Susie Bill, a red Fetcher, and Ben her stable mate, a smooth black Satin Crammer, always took up their positions on a chair by the window a quarter of an hour before their master returned home – whatever time he arrived. As he worked eight miles away, it was as though they sensed the exact time he left work. When Mr Bill's mother died, he went over to her house to sort out her things, telling his wife he'd be home by seven. During the afternoon he rang to say, there was so much

Kim Spink

201

to do he wouldn't be back until long after nine. At six forty-five, the dogs took up their lookout positions on their chair.

'You'll have a long wait,' warned Mrs Bill, but sure enough at seven o'clock Mr Bill arrived, having decided to abandon sorting for the day and come home after all.

The sceptic would insist that the dogs recognize the sound of their owner's car, and also have far superior hearing to humans, but surely this hearing would not be acute enough to pick up a car leaving a quarter of an hour's drive away. Nor does this explain the behaviour of a Rough Diamond called Judy Brown, who lives in a shop where cars are pulling up all day, but who only barks at her master's car, although she can't see him arriving from inside the shop. Nor is it the sound of the engine she recognizes, as she barked the first time he turned up in a new car. She also barks before the telephone rings.

Another inexplicable phenomenon is the mongrel's ability to select the right bus. Bully Latchford, a stalwart Prop Forward from Wimbledon, like many a man before him got bored when he was taken shopping by his mistress and used to sneak off and take the 93 bus home. He always went upstairs and was a great favourite with the conductors. He knew it was time to get off when the bus levelled out at the top of the hill, but, and this is the remarkable part, although there were two bus routes from the town shops, Bully always caught the right bus.

Miss Ellen Coath, who worked as a governess in Beckenham before the war, also remembers a Bertrand Russell called Bobby who was a great wanderer. He used to take free bus rides from the village, to the end of the road, where Miss Coath lived. One day when she was already on the bus, she saw him board it, run upstairs, crawl under a front seat, then jump out at the right stop. There were two buses which took different routes from Beckenham, but Bobby, like Bully, always took the right one.

Even more impressive at the turn of the century were the navigational skills of a mongrel called Kruger Rogerson.

'He was owned by my dad's Uncle Jim,' writes Mr Rogerson, 'who was a road paver and always took Kruger to work. Each morning Uncle Jim caught a Stockport tram from Cheadle Heath to Mersey Square in the centre of Stockport, changed trams to take another six mile ride to Hyde Town Hall, then caught a train to Mottram. On several occasions Kruger overslept after a night on the tiles, but nothing daunted would set off, catch all the necessary connections, and get to work only half an hour after his master. All the conductors knew him. On his collar was stamped, "I am Kruger Rogerson, who the hell are you?"'

Bobby Coath

202

When Mrs Margaret Turner was a child before the war, she had a little Terrier called Raggy who always picked her up on time from school, and whose bump of locality was as good as his time clock. Every Saturday night he took a train to the other side of Huddersfield to visit an old lady who gave him chocolate biscuits, then caught the right train home again. It must have been easier for dogs in those days when there was less traffic, and no one kicked up a queenie fuss if a stray dog joined them in a bus or train carriage. Raggy's bump of locality also stood him in good stead during a family outing, when he got lost on the moors seven miles from home. Margaret sobbed and sobbed, thinking she'd never see her dog again, but when the family got back home there was Raggy wagging on the doorstep. He was probably guided home by scent, but there are extraordinary tales of dogs finding their way home after travelling to a strange place by car.

Bobby, a two-and-a-half-year-old mongrel belonging to a French florist in the town of La Ferté Alais, got lost in the flower market in the heart of Paris. After a fruitless search his master returned sadly home. Yet five days later an exhausted Bobby arrived on the doorstep. He had covered thirty-five miles and, even more impressive, this rural dog had found his way out of Paris, one of the busiest and most geographically complicated cities in the world.

Dogs who travel to a place by car must notice landmarks on the way. During the war Mr Sharpe, who lived in Finchley, used to drive the family and their dog Chum along a labyrinth of back roads to visit his in-laws in Wood Green. One day Chum, a sleek Standard Magpie with the inevitable badger streak down his forehead, vanished after a bitch. The family searched everywhere, but like the French florist had to return home to Finchley empty-handed. At two-thirty in the morning they were overjoyed to hear a faint scratch on the back door. Bedraggled, exhausted and desperately thirsty, Chum had come the fifteen miles home.

Sometimes by returning to base by a circuitous route a stray mongrel wins its spurs and is allowed to stay. Mr Hutchings tells a touching story of the Standard Magpie bitch he and his sister found wandering in Brixton market when they were children.

Chum Sharpe

'We were convinced it was Floss, our neighbour's bitch. She wagged her tail so hard when we called her that we found an old piece of rope and took her home by tram. When we reached our neighbour's house she was amazed, because her own Floss was already in residence. We realized the two pups were identical. Mother insisted we took our Floss back to Brixton, so tearfully we boarded the tram and took her back to market. We kept looking back hoping she might follow us, but she didn't. To our delight, when we got home we found her waiting. Mother relented, and she became a member of our family for ten years.'

Whatever good fairy guided Floss and the other dogs back home was aided by the fact that the dogs had been to the place at least once before. Michael Fox, in his book *Understanding your Dog*, suggests that some dogs may have a homing instinct, like carrier pigeons, and are able to navigate by the angle of the sun or the stars. If a dog is separated from home (or the place he considers he ought to be) his internal clock tells him there is an incongruity between the time of day he feels inside him, and the time of day the sun is registering by virtue of its position. He then sets out in the direction that will reduce this internal and external difference. Once he gets near home, he will pick up familiar smells and sights and find his way more easily.

What is far more difficult to explain is how dogs trace owners to places where the dog has never been. There was for example a mongrel in the First World War who, never having been out of England before, crossed the channel and found his master in the trenches. Then there was the mongrel called Tony, who was left in the care of friends because his owners had moved from Illinois to a town in Michigan some 225 miles away. Somehow, six weeks later, Tony, wearing his identifying collar and disc, turned up at the Michigan home. Such feats must defy the rational mind and it is here we enter the tricky world of ESP or 'Psi-trailing', as it is called, which means the psychic location of where someone is. Perhaps in the same way that the mongrel in Australia 'knew' his mistress had landed, Tony and the dog in the First World War were drawn by some sixth sense to their owners. T. S. Eliot wrote of lovers 'who think the same thoughts without need of speech.' Perhaps dogs, whose devotion exceeds that of most lovers, are able to pick up telepathetic vibrations from beloved owners who are constantly thinking and worrying about them.

Apart from being able to find their owners, some dogs seem to be able to see into the future. It is standard practice for mongrel owners to feel their dogs know exactly what they are going to do before they do it. Others said that if ever they visited friends on foot, their dog would always lead them to the house where they wanted to go – even though they had many friends they often visited in that same road.

204

Collies, as has already been pointed out, seem particularly psychic. Lassie Halliwell, a Family Circler, and her mistress were going down a blind alley-way leading into a country lane. Suddenly Lassie, who usually bounded ahead, sat down and refused to budge. As her mistress turned back to get her, a car shot across the entrance of the alley-way, steered by a man who'd been up on a dangerous driving charge a week before. If Mrs Halliwell hadn't stopped for Lassie, she would certainly have been run over.

An even more eerie tale of canine premonition was sent in by Mrs Stride whose father owned a fish-curing business in Balta-sound at the turn of the century. Among his fishing fleet was a boat called the *Jeannie Inglis*, whose crew of five men had a little Bertrand Russell with a badger streak called Nellie, who always sailed with them however rough the weather. She never roamed, but one day when the boat was putting out to sea, she bolted inland and couldn't be found, so the *Jeannie Inglis* sailed without her. Wise Nellie – the boat was never seen again, and not one bit of wreckage was ever found. Seas can be very treach-erous in the winter in this part and there was no power then, only sails. In Baltasound to this day, people still talk about the mystery of the *Jeannie Inglis*. Happily poor Nellie didn't starve; Mrs Stride's family adopted her.

Perhaps Nellie had a premonition of death. Mrs Burchell of Oxford observed similar behaviour in Stumpy, her father's Black and Tan Tightskin.

'One day,' she writes, 'my father came home feeling very ill. The doctor diagnosed pneumonia. For five days he fought for his life, all the time calling repeatedly for Stumpy. But she refused to enter his bedroom. On the sixth day, the doctor announced the crisis was over, and my father was out of danger. Everyone rejoiced. I was about to take Stumpy for a much deserved walk. Suddenly she whimpered, dashed up-stairs to my father's bedroom, and jumping on the bed franti-cally licked his face. He was so pleased to see her. It was as much as I could do to drag her out for her walk. Within the hour, my father died.'

Other mongrels can sense that a person they love is in trouble from miles away. Chip Smith, yet another Black and Tan Tight-skin, frequently stays with friends when his master is working away from home. Chip always settles in quite happily, having the good manners to pull his weight as a guest wherever he goes. On one occasion, however, when he was staying with other people, his master was taken ill and rushed to hospital.

205

Although Chip couldn't see his master he realized he was in danger, and howled and whined, and refused to settle. The moment his master was off the danger list, however, the little dog stopped worrying and relaxed.

Nimbus Sangster, another psychic Family Circler with gold flyaway ears, was particularly attached to one of her mistress's friends, who lived in Yorkshire but who often came to stay with the Sangsters in Essex. On returning to Yorkshire after a visit the friend became ill, but no one realized how seriously – except Nimbus, who suddenly one evening became terribly distressed and started howling, a thing she'd never done before. Next morning Mrs Sangster had a call to say that her friend had had a stroke, just at the time Nimbus had started howling the night before. She died a few hours later. How did Nimbus know someone she loved was dying 300 miles away?

Nimbus Sangster

Yet another Borderline Collie, Cindy Loo Morgan, also had second sight. One foggy night when her mistress was due home from work, Cindy suddenly started to howl. Nothing seemed physically wrong with her; her master checked her water bowl, and opened the door for her to go out, but the howling continued. Then the telephone rang. It was Mrs Morgan.

'You've had a crash,' her husband told her.

'How did you know?' she asked.

'Because Cindy told me.'

Mrs Morgan fortunately was not seriously hurt, but the car was badly dented. If anyone in the family was in trouble, Cindy always seemed to sense it. Later on when her master was taken to hospital, Mrs Morgan came home to be with her step-son John. Cindy sat shivering between them. At exactly ten minutes past ten, she licked first Mrs Morgan's face, then John's, then gave a great howl. The next minute, the hospital rang to say Mr Morgan had died.

Sceptics would no doubt say that Cindy and Nimbus had picked up anxiety vibrations from their owners. But what made them howl suddenly when no one else in the house was remotely aware death was so close?

I have received many letters from people who told me they had seen ghosts of their dogs – perhaps we should call them monghouls. One woman had been informed by a spiritualist that her dog was still with her, while one man sent me a faded snapshot in which you can see the faint shadowy ghost of his Collie Cymri beside the grave.

The most extraordinary letter however came from a Mrs Anderson of Cheshire, whose adored golden Tightskin, Jen,

206

died last year at the age of fourteen. The Andersons were all set to buy another dog, when suddenly and inexplicably Mrs Anderson got cold feet and decided to put it off for another week. Coming home from work the next evening, she opened the front door:

'There was Jen to greet me, I actually did see her. I'm not a crank, the supernatural's not a hobby of mine. And as naturally as if she were alive, I bent to stroke her, and found nothing there. Thinking the family would feel I'd gone off my head, I kept quiet about the incident.'

The following evening, however, Mrs Anderson was sitting with her husband in the drawing-room when they heard a rustle of newspapers. Two papers then fell out of the rack, and were actually moving around on the floor in exactly the manner that Jen pushed them when she wanted to make a bed.

'Hullo, Jen,' said Mr Anderson. Immediately the paper stopped rustling and they both knew she was there. They decided not to tell the children about this, but a week later their youngest daughter said, 'Don't think I'm going dotty, Mum, but our Jen's been on my bed. There was a dent in the pillow, and it was warm to touch, and I heard Jen jumping off the bed, just as I entered the room.'

Jen has been dead for six months now, but the Andersons are convinced she is always with them, an 'affable familiar ghost' who still feels she is guarding them, and who would be jealous of anyone else muscling in on her territory.

'Until the feeling has disappeared,' writes Mrs Anderson, 'we cannot bring ourselves to get another pet.'

Chapter 25

Heinz super dogs

One of my favourite cartoons is of Fred Basset watching a large dog passing this house, and musing to himself, 'That's a Great Dane, but not a great Great Dane.' This penultimate chapter is devoted to four great great dogs, three dead, one still alive, who seem to encapsulate those essential mongrel virtues of character, heart, intelligence, loyalty and a true zest for life.

We begin on the outskirts of Bury St Edmunds in the twenties, with Old Jack Pratt, a fine Rough and Reddish, who had the typically mongrel intelligence to choose a butcher for a master.

Jack Pratt

My father worked late hours at the shop [writes Miss Pratt] so he bought Mum a dog to protect her when she was alone with just us children in the house. Old Jack was a handsome terrier with a tufted ginger and brown coat, and dark brown ears and muzzle. He would lie on Mum's feet in the evening, and at the slightest noise rush to the front door baring his teeth, hair sticking up like a porcupine. True to his terrier ancestry, he was the fighting terror of all the neighbourhood, and would tackle anything many times his size, but was terrified of thunder, and would creep into the tiny cupboard where Mum kept her sewing machine. He was marvellous with children. Our parents had no fear of letting us wander in the country. Old Jack never left our side, he was the equivalent of a whole Corps of Securicor guards.

Old Jack Pratt may have eaten no fat, but he certainly realized the value of protein. The Pratt family kept chickens. Mr Pratt couldn't understand why his usually tidy wife chucked shells all over the lawn. The mystery was solved when Jack was observed crawling into the hen run, extracting an egg from one of the nests, then sitting on the lawn holding it between his paws, carefully cracking it and sucking out the meat like a Shakespearean fool.

209

Old Jack thought the world of Dad [continues Miss Pratt] and although he never admitted it, Dad reciprocated. A hard worker, Dad liked his mid-morning pint when the shop wasn't busy. Jack often went to the shop to see Dad, and if he wasn't there, looked for him in all the local bars. If Mum took Jack shopping, she often embarrassingly found herself being towed on a compulsory pub crawl.

The greatest comedy, however, came when the cinema opposite the butcher's shop opened a bar, which was very handy if Mr Pratt fancied a quick morning snort. This haunt soon became known to Old Jack. One evening when Mr Pratt was in his office balancing the books, an irate cinema manager barged in demanding that he remove his dog.

During the matinée Jack had evidently popped into the bar in search of his master, and, not finding him there, had settled into a comfortable double courting seat in the 'two and nines'. He obviously wanted to watch the programme through a second time because he growled off all the attempts by alarmed usherettes to evict him.

It was a black day for the family when Jack began to fail. His coat became thin and patchy. His lovely brown eyes clouded, the vet diagnosed stomach cancer , and he was put to sleep.

'My parents swore we would never replace Jack,' writes Miss Pratt 'but canine loyalty and companionship are something you grow into. Within a week, Dad came home with a pedigree Fox Terrier puppy, like one Mum had admired in a magazine. Gyp was pretty and lovable, and soon won all our hearts, but he lacked the irrepressible fire and stamina of poor dear brave Jack, who will never be forgotten by any of us. Dad died two years ago. At eighty-eight, only weeks before he died, he retailed for the umpteenth time his favourite tale of how Jack got stuck in the two and nines. Perhaps up there they are united. I like to think so.'

We move to wartime, and the second great mongrel: Major Olins, a tan and white Family Circler, with a white streak running down his face, and a long plumy tail. The Major was also a military camp follower for food not love, surviving the first year of his life attached to an army camp near London and living on scraps from the kitchen. When the regiment moved on it was decided to put the Major down, but a tenderhearted officer took the dog home to his sister, Diana, who was living in Streatham and working for the ARP. Diana was then in her twenties, unmarried, and busy putting out fires in the district,

Major Olins

210

which was at that time being peppered with 'V2' rockets. Food was very scarce. Reluctantly she agreed to keep the Major overnight. He decided to stay with her for fourteen and a half years.

After being wounded in two air-raids, and being bombed out thrice, the Major moved with his mistress to a house in Streatham where she installed a shelter in the dining-room. The Major always anticipated raids and was the first into the shelter, barking for everyone to hurry. Despite the bombs, the Major never lost his passion for soldiers. Whenever convoys came by he would jump into the lorries, cover anything clad in khaki with great slobbery kisses, and hitch a lift for a few miles.

Apart from his regular success in raising army morale, he was also called in on one occasion to clear a nearby bomb crater of rats, and twice got his name in the *Streatham News*. He then slightly blotted his copybook by falling in love with a bitch from a nearby pre-fab. When she produced five puppies (the image of the Major even to his freckles) the irate owner issued him with a paternity suit, and demanded food for the offspring. Consequently the Major's mistress had to queue for whale meat every day to keep the owner quiet. Nor was the owner very amused when the Major sent the bitch a brass curtain ring, and a letter signed with a grubby paw from his solicitors Airedale, Airedale and Alsatian Ltd to say the Major would do all he could to help, but didn't accept full liability.

After the war, the Major supervised the family's move to Hove, and settled into a slightly more normal and up-market life. As there were no lorries available, he used to hitch rides on the white open-top buses to Rottingdean every day, and this time made the *Brighton Argus*. Another favourite haunt was Zetland's, the famous cake shop in Hove. The Major developed a passion for their almond biscuits, and would sit outside uttering pathetic groans like a junkie and refusing all other offerings.

In his declining years, an old retired Major, he lived on scrambled eggs, and loved to sit in the sun. His mistress made him a yellow sunhat which he fetched in his mouth to be tied on his head when the weather was hot and when he wanted to meditate, no doubt, on his beginnings as a camp follower, his sexual peccadillos, his press cuttings, and finally life by the sea.

Moving into the early sixties we come to another Major, Major Hugo of Corsham, Wiltshire, a splendid chestnut and white Prop Forward with a wise white face, glistening black nose, and jaunty S-bend tail with a white tip.

'We had just lost our previous mongrel,' writes Miss Hugo,   Major Hugo

211

'when my mother saw Major in the local market. He had nothing to recommend him except one closed eye and a suit that looked a few sizes too big for him.' Abandoning her shopping, she brought him home in a carrier bag and in no time had him tucked up in the old dog's basket with several blankets and a hot-water bottle.

The Hugos soon discovered Major was not only being eaten alive by worms, but also had an inverted eyelid. Only days of careful nursing, and later an eye operation, pulled him through. He rewarded their kindness with great loyalty, and by growing into a tremendous character who didn't miss a trick.

If Miss Hugo or her parents wore anything new or changed the rooms around, Major spotted it immediately and was in there investigating. He also had a sixth sense about squeaky toys, smelling them out even if they were at the bottom of a shopping bag, and wrapped in paper and two layers of polythene. It was impossible to smuggle in a Christmas present for him.

'One day,' writes Miss Hugo, 'we bought a garden gnome and put it in the middle of the kitchen floor for Major to inspect. He was very wary and circled it at a distance. Finally he put out a paw, then gingerly nudged it with his nose. When he found it didn't squeak he lost interest, apart from giving it a few funny looks.'

Major's eating habits were bizarre. He always refused tinned food, preferring to share the family's joints of meat. 'Nor did he like the same meat on consecutive days,' writes Miss Hugo. 'We felt pork was his least favourite. He liked his vegetables with plenty of gravy. In summer, if we were having a salad and mother felt it was too hot to cook just for Major, he'd eat a hard-boiled egg, but only if it was mashed up with butter. He went to bed with a polo mint each night, but was careful to wash his mouth out afterwards with a drink of water.'

Major was equally fastidious about his medicine. After one holiday, he came back from the kennels with a cough, so the Hugos gave him Victory V lozenges, Hacks and a spoonful of honey. He'd take anything that humans took, but refused to touch dog cough linctus.

As the Hugos lived in a bungalow they could leave their bedroom doors open and hear Major at night.

'Mother told him that if he needed her, he should come and fetch her. Sometimes he became frightened when he found he couldn't stop coughing, and would go into the bedroom and give her a thump on the back with his paws. She would immedi-

212

ately get up and give him a butter mint to settle his cough.' Several times the canny Major was heard to climb out of bed, nudge his mistress awake and then put on a very convincing display of coughing in order to get his butter mint.

To relieve his cough, Mrs Hugo used to form a pillow for Major's head when she settled him down. He soon realized the benefit of this, and began deliberately piling up his bedding to make a pillow. One New Year's Eve, Major began to bleed, and the vet diagnosed prostate trouble but said he was too old for an operation. In February he lost the use of his legs. His family couldn't see so grand a dog suffer, so they had him put to sleep.

'We consider ourselves extremely lucky to have had Major,' adds Miss Hugo. 'It will take us a long time to get over his loss, if in fact we ever do; it's been like losing a child.'

Finally we come to a great modern mongrel, Jason Parker of Eddlesborough, (see p. 208), who looks with his wise Terrier face and rough black and tan coat more like a pre-war dog.

'Our Jason,' writes Mrs Parker, 'is loyal, intelligent, faithful and kind. We never had to train him; everything he does is instinctive. He has never chewed up anything, and never snapped or bitten even when run over by a bicycle.'

This paragon of virtues also never needs a lead, never attacks other pets, loves thunder and fireworks, adores all children and never fights other dogs. He will wait outside any shop. Once when he had been forgotten, he waited for four hours outside Marks and Spencer. At midnight, when his mistress is ready to leave work, she dials home and lets the phone buzz twice. Then her husband lets Jason out, and he races to meet her and accompanies her home.

Jason never steals, stoically enters fancy dress competitions without grumbling, has taught himself to swim; hates any of the family getting wet and tries to lick them dry; guards the pram; is first to the bedside at night if any of the children cry. He is also a good camper, keeps to the pavement when the family are riding bikes, and loves the slide in the playground.

'Jason always left home,' concludes Mrs Parker, 'to get to my son's playgroup twenty minutes early, so he could sit in the ring with the children and listen to their story and singsong. At ten o'clock every day, he joins the local workmen for tea and sandwiches. He is a fine guard dog, he never gets on furniture. He is gentle and good – and we wouldn't swap him for the world.'

Chapter 26

Old age and death

Soda was the sparkle in our lives for sixteen years. We held her tightly to the end.

Mrs Walton of Amersham

The mongrel grows old. His stomach sags. His eyes grow smaller, his teeth yellow, his coloured coat is threaded with white. He is less anxious to go for walks and tends to lie in in the morning. Some dogs remain active right to the end. At the great age of twenty, Coon Carruthers, a beautiful brown and white Rough Diamond, still retained her slender figure and merry ways and accompanied her mistress to school every day. Peter Ferris, at twenty-one-and-a-half the oldest dog in the book, looked a mere stripling in the photograph taken a few weeks before he died. While Miquette Czernin, an adorable black Romney Marshall, who nearly died of distemper as a tiny puppy, has now clocked up a commendable eighteen and a half years. Recently she survived a long and difficult move from Edinburgh to London, loves her food, can still jump on the bed, and seems to enjoy life.

'She is the sweetest natured, most devoted, loyal and humble dog I have ever owned,' writes her mistress. 'I cannot say how much I dread the day when she will be no longer with me.'

Coon Carruthers

To keep a dog alive when it is old and suffering is sheer selfishness, but many mongrels adjust to infirmity extremely well. One example was Gretchen Handover, a beautiful Hover Cur. She was healthy at sixteen except for a heart condition which prompted the vet to put her on digitalis. Every day when it was time for her pill, Gretchen would remind her mistress by sitting at her feet and opening her mouth in anticipation.

Mrs Bootle lived in a cottage with almost vertical stairs. Both of her bitches developed bad arthritis in their legs. One of them used to hurtle down the stairs hardly touching the steps, which

Gretchen Handover

215

Peter Ferris

did her no good as she got older, so she learnt to come down one step at a time, carefully placing her back feet on the next stair down just as her front feet moved off it onto the next one. When the other bitch, at the age of fourteen, grew too heavy to be carried upstairs, Mrs Bootle taught her to go up by bunny jumping.

Mrs Mary York of Cornwall also tells the hilarious story of one of her father's parishioners who owned a very fat Half Cocker called Robbie, who always slept on her bed. Sadly, she overfed him, so he became fatter and fatter until he could no longer leap on the bed – and she was too frail to lift him. After much pondering, the old lady suddenly remembered the previous year's nativity play, and the wooden steps used by the three kings to mount the stage majestically. She asked the vicar – 'who never refused anyone anything' – if she could have the steps. The next day they were placed beside her bed. Robbie examined them suspiciously for a long time, then sustained by much encouragement he got the message and up he went.

When little Stumpy Burchell, the Bertrand Russell with second sight, grew old, she went blind. She coped very well in her own house and garden when there was somebody about. but pined when she was left at home on her own. She also got very muddled and frightened by all the feet of the passers-by when she was taken into the town on a lead.

Fortunately a friend gave Mrs Burchell a regular Rolls-Royce pram complete with canopy and silken fringe, big enough for a dozen Stumpies. On further investigation, Mrs Burchell discovered a panel that could be raised a foot from the head of the pram to support a baby when it sits up. The space behind was just the right size for Stumpy, who rode in splendour for her remaining years.

Throwing out a dog on a motorway at any age is criminal, but anyone who dumps a faithful old dog when it starts to fail ought to be hung, drawn and quartered. Fortunately the Canine Defence League allows the public to sponsor dogs as kennel pensioners that are too old or too disturbed when they are brought in to be placed with a new family. Early in 1979 Fred, a black and tan mongrel, was found wandering on the M4. He was taken to the Newbury Canine Defence Kennels, where they found he was not only a very ancient dog, but blind in one eye and deaf as well. Despite the appalling traumas he must have suffered on the edge of a busy motorway, he seems to love his new home and has many friends in the OAP block.

Sandie Woodrow, the blonde Spanish Policeman's Hat Ear

Dog, is now thirteen, and like Fred she often gets confused. 'Food is her big interest,' writes her mistress. 'She doesn't walk far now although snow still has the power to rejuvenate her. She snores and yelps in her dreams, but remains our most treasured possession. She will only be put down if her life seems to have lost its savour.'

The trouble with mongrels is that they are so stoical it is difficult to tell how much they are suffering. Spike Mayers was doted on by his master and mistress to such an extent that when Mrs Mayers had her first baby, she was convinced Spike was sulking because he always shuffled three yards behind the pram whenever she took out the baby. It was only when Spike was taken critically ill that the vet discovered he was dying of an ulcer which must have been active for some time.

'We could only wonder,' writes Mrs Mayers, 'at the great loyalty and love he had shown by managing to struggle that far.'

Laddy Jaques, unknown to his owners, had cancer. He must have been in excruciating pain, but still managed when one member of the family got married to stagger a mile and a half to visit her every day; he would then flop down exhausted, girding his strength for the return journey.

In the same way, mongrels want to make things easier for their owners by playing down the agony of death. 'I'm so sorry to be a bother,' they seem to say with their last breath, 'I'm all right, please don't worry.' Peter Booth, a splendidly jovial Standard Magpie, staggered to meet his mistress wagging his tail, and with a toy in his mouth, the day he died. While Littlewood, Daniel Farson's beloved Borderline Collie, licked his hand reassuringly as, blinded by tears, he left her with the vet to be put down.

Bob Giles, the great swimmer and holiday-maker, developed cancer when he was nearly sixteen. 'He was in such frightful pain,' wrote Mrs Giles, 'that we took the dreadful decision to have him put down. My in-laws were staying. As my husband and I reached the door, I said, "Say good-bye to Nanny." Bob trotted through the hall and right to the end of the lounge, licked Mum's face and then Dad's, and then came back to me. We were all broken-hearted, as he was still wagging his tail and, as my younger daughter used to say "smiling"'

Tim Jowett, the gorgeous Rough Diamond who reacted so strongly to 'Silent Night', died when he was twelve. Nothing in his life became him like the leaving of it. 'As I waited for the vet to take him away,' writes Mrs Jowett, 'I put up my ironing board. Tim at once tried to drag himself to lie beneath it as he

Tim Jowett

217

always did. No matter how much I tripped over him and grumbled, he would always stay there till I finished. This time he simply couldn't make it, so he just looked at me with dumb apology. A very nice lady came for him. What a lovely dog, she said, as she gently carried him to her van. I couldn't see for the tears, as I waved good-bye to a true and faithful friend, who had so bravely tried to do his duty with his last remaining strength.'

Happily many mongrels die from natural causes. Mrs Poxon bought a long sofa on which her grandsons could all watch television. Willie, her Satin Crammer, had other ideas and commandeered the whole sofa so that there was never any room for anyone else. He also died peacefully on it at the age of sixteen.

Sally Hart, the brindle Rough-and-Reddish who was 'so ordinary looking that no one else wanted her,' died at sixteen completely one of the family. One night she had trouble with her breathing and whined slightly, then suddenly, as if she knew it was the end, she threw back her head, gave a great howl and died. Prince Samson, the Satin Crammer who was never ill, lived to a ripe old age. He just met Mrs Thomson at the gate one day, tried to bark his delight at her return, then lay down at her feet and died.

Maggie Darwin

One of the most beautiful and gentle-natured mongrels, a black Lurcher with a white shirt front called Maggie Darwin, died of a heart attack when she was only six, chasing a hare round her own courtyard. When a dog dies so young, one is left with a sense of outrage that she never lived out her appointed span. Mongrel owners are lucky in this respect, because their dogs tend to live much longer than breed dogs. (If dog years had been calculated on a mongrel life expectancy of about fourteen years, rather than the ten years of a pedigree dog, the ratio would be reduced to five dog years for one human year.) But when death finally comes to the beloved mongrel after sixteen, seventeen, or even twenty-one years, it is all the more agonizing. The relationship has lasted longer than many marriages and most childhoods, and whereas husbands and wives are generally separated during the day, and children go off to school and often leave home at sixteen, a dog is your constant companion, if you will let him be, day in day out. No wonder the wrench is terrible.

'The misery of keeping a dog is his dying so soon,' wrote Walter Scott. 'But to be sure if he lived fifty years, and then died, what would become of me?'

Scott had many dogs but his favourite was a mongrel, a Bulldog Terrier cross called Camp, whose loyalty and intelligence made up for any lack of looks. Scott was quite inconsolable at his death. According to his son-in-law, he buried Camp on a fine moonlit night in the little garden behind the house in Castle Street, below the window where he usually wrote. All the family were in tears as Scott himself smoothed down the turf above Camp, with the saddest expression on his face his daughter had ever seen. He had been engaged to dine abroad that day, but apologized on account of the death of a dear old friend. And Mr McDonald, his host, was not at all surprised that he should have done so, when it came out next morning that Camp was no more.

One of the most heartbreaking aspects of writing this book was that every week I got letters from owners who'd already written to me, telling me their mongrels were no more. Sally Keay, the Satin Crammer from Liverpool, fretted herself to death, pining for her dead kennel mate. Sam Hamilton, chief howler and mighty warrior, went in November. Little Lucy Hanbury-Aggs, a doughty Jack Russell/Pekinese cross after surviving several operations for cancer finally died in December.

Mr Heller, a young Lancastrian, had been off sick for two years after an accident. His sole companion while his wife was out at work was Tiny, the original Lancashire Hot Pet. Just as Mr Heller was starting to walk again, and was looking forward to taking Tiny out once more, the dog died of a heart attack on Christmas night. Here is part of a letter Mr Heller wrote me on New Year's Eve:

'I play back his bark on a tape recorder, and talk to him. It is New Year's Night, a cold wind is blowing a gale, lots of Christmas paper and New Year's trimmings float about our road. I gaze at the settee and cry my eyes out for a game little creature who did not want to give up, sorry but tears have landed on your letter.'

'When Dusty died aged twelve years,' wrote Mrs Cantle, 'it was just like losing one of the family. Even my twenty-eight-year-old son sat with tears in his eyes.'

Dusty Cantle

Some owners derive comfort from how much other people loved their dog. 'For fourteen years we had the unquestioning devotion of this magnificent dog,' wrote Mrs Bell of the Isle of Wight about her Borderline Collie, Rover. 'Few humans could leave more sadness than he did when he died. All the local children brought posies to his grave.'

Other people bottle it up. 'The day my dog Lassie had to be put down,' according to one ITN cameraman, 'was the blackest day of my life. Even years later I have not come to terms with it. I

219

have never had the last photographs I took of her developed, or ever spoken to anyone of her death before.'

How does one get over such grief? I suspect it is easier if you have a grave at which to mourn. Mr Smith buried his adored wayward Ebony Fetcher Pancho on the hills near his home, and every time a coat wears out, he makes a pilgrimage to the spot and lays it on the grave.

T.H.White, the novelist, owned a Red Setter, called Brownie, and was distraught when she died. 'I stayed near the grave for a week, so I could go out once or twice a day, and say, "Good girl, sleepy girl, go to sleep, Brownie." It was a saying she understood, and I said it steadily. I suppose the chance of consciousness persisting for a week is several million to one, but that was the chance I had to provide for.'

'Toby struggled with arthritis and heart trouble,' wrote Mrs Hall. 'Then one day he just looked up at me and said, "I have had twelve and a half years of life, now let me go." In July 1979 he was put to sleep. He now lies at rest with pedigree dogs in Silvermere Pet cemetery, you're all the same once you're dead. On his gravestone is engraved, "He speaketh not and yet there lies a conversation in his eyes."'

Battersea Dogs' Home tells an endearing story of an old man living on the edge of Wimbledon Common who was so devoted to Scruff, the mongrel he rescued, that he had the dog stuffed when it died. When the old man died a few years later, his widow had him and the stuffed Scruff buried together in the same coffin – rather like the stone Greyhound crouching at the feet of the armoured knight.

One of the most agonizing decisions is how to fill this terrible gap in one's life left by the death of a beloved dog. Mrs Gornall was so heartbroken she never tried:

'Patch was the only dog we've ever had. We bought him from the local RSPCA and carried him home in a shopping basket. He died at thirteen. He was the best friend I've ever had, and all for fifteen shillings.'

Miss de Lory was so upset when her irrepressible Romney Marshall, Bouncer, died that it was four years before she felt able to get another puppy. She was young and had time on her side. Sadly, some old age pensioners feel it would be unfair to get another mongrel because it might outlive them and be left homeless once again. Others either live in houses where dogs aren't allowed, or simply can't afford them.

'My last dog Lady was a lovely pet,' wrote seventy-four-year-old Mrs Barker. 'I miss her very much, and I still have a weep

220

when I think of her. We thought it best not to have another dog. The bills are so high and we only have our pension.'

Other owners feel it is disloyal to the memory of the dog that has just died to try and replace it, or that they couldn't subject themselves to the misery of another death.

'I am lonely for just another reservoir for my love,' wrote T. H. White after Brownie died, 'but if I did get such a reservoir, it would die in about twelve years, and at present I feel I couldn't face it.'

Fortunately his friend David Garnett wrote back urging him to get another dog: 'The best antidote to the numbing obsession of grief is having responsibility for a living creature; often it will hurt you, but you will realize you cannot dodge the responsibility.'

I am convinced that if possible one should get another dog immediately. When my own lovely Setter, Maidstone, had to be put down, Fortnum did his loyal utmost to comfort me, but I didn't really get over the loss until five months later when Fortnum's daughter Mabel came to live with us, and I once again had something small and helpless to occupy my time.

One of the first letters I received from a mongrel owner when researching this book was from a Mrs Spice, who told me that her Black and Tan Tightskin, Toby, had just died. This was her second letter:

'Dear Jilly, You said my letter made you cry and hoped we'd soon find another mongrel. Well, we have. Yillah is seven weeks old, and amazingly is identical in marking and colour to Toby. Apart from having a white chin, and being a bitch, she could be him. I wonder how many owners choose a similar type of dog to the previous one – it might be an interesting topic to pursue.'

When man is lonely, wrote Lamartine, God sends him a dog.

Aware of Mr Heller's utter desolation at Christmas when Tiny died, I was thrilled on 28 February to get a letter from him enclosing photographs of their new puppy, Tiny II, who is the image of the old dog.

'We got him from the dogs' home,' wrote Mr Heller. 'He had worms, sore eyes, and intestine disorder, but was so appealing and like our first Tiny that my wife could not resist bringing him home. The lady at the dogs' home did not charge the usual £10. I think she thought he'd had it. Now he looks as fit as a butcher's dog.'

Like all good mongrel stories, this one ended with a happy beginning.

Tiny Heller II.

Tiny Heller I

Tel
Horndean. 59...

...Warden
...dal Close
...laen
...tsmouth
P.O8. 8ET.

Dear Tilly

Your letter in Daily Mail 23/7/50
brought back a flood of memories of a little
dog I had, I had many proofs of his intelligence and loyalty.

I remember my husband had a
load of Farm manure placed the length of a
garden bed, Peter (that was his name) did not approve
of this - So he covered it over with earth using
his nose as a shovel.

When I had a sta... ...
in hospital, he ...
that he could one...
his legs refused ...
in Woolworths one...
to be there — he...
Woolworths, which ...
and a window betw...
on the edge of the ...
and he watched ev...
either door. When we...
fetch his brush, comb...
felt our things.
We had him for 16 ys...
which no other dog coul...
three breed dogs since ...

LLOYD'S
LIME STREET.
LONDON, EC3M 7HL

... Hills Cottage,
...oxwood,
West Sussex
...uly 1950

... have met
... me you were
... girls.

... ...pes of strange -
looking ones and I enclose herewith
two photographs of each which may
be of interest — They are good
natured if nothing else!

I gather Felise and our
Simon are due to go to Hamish